WHALES

and other Marine Mammals *of*
BRITISH COLUMBIA
and
ALASKA

Tamara Eder

illustrations by
Ian Sheldon

with technical contributions from
Don Pattie

Lone Pine Publishing

The Publisher: Lone Pine Publishing
10145 – 81 Ave.   1901 Raymond Ave. SW, Suite C
Edmonton, AB T6E 1W9   Renton, WA 98055
Canada   USA
Website: http://www.lonepinepublishing.com

National Library of Canada Cataloguing in Publication Data
Eder, Tamara, (date)
    Whales and other marine mammals of British Columbia and Alaska

    Includes bibliographical references and index.
    ISBN 1-55105-268-7

    1. Whales—British Columbia—Identification. 2. Whales—Alaska—
Identification. 3. Marine mammals—British Columbia—Identification.
4. Marine mammals—Alaska—Identification. I. Sheldon, Ian, (date)
II. Title.
QL737.C4E232 2001   599.5'09711   C2001-910040-X

Editorial Director: Nancy Foulds
Project Editor: Roland Lines
Technical Review: Ian McCaskie
Production Manager: Jody Reekie
Cover Design: Robert Weidemann
Book Design: Robert Weidemann
Layout & Production: Ian Dawe
Cartography: Robert Weidemann, Ian Dawe
Cover Illustrations: Striped Dolphin, Humpback Whale, Minke Whale by Ian Sheldon

Photograph Credits
The photographs in this book are reproduced with the generous permission of their copyright holders. Ken Balcomb, pp. 40 & 94; Corel Corporation (photos by Eric Stoops), pp. 44, 52, 74, 78, 98 & 112; Renee DeMartin/West Stock, pp. 56, 88 & 130; Tamara Eder, p. 150; Eyewire, p. 120; David B. Fleetham/ Visuals Unlimited, p. 68; Mark Newman/West Stock, pp. 126 & 146; Nada Pecnik/Visuals Unlimited, p. 136; Marty Snyderman/Visuals Unlimited, p. 60; Jack Stephens, p. 142

Additional Illustrations
The illustrations of the two otters (pp. 148 & 152) are by Gary Ross.

We acknowledge the financial support of the Government of Canada through the Book Publishing Industry Development Program (BPIDP) for our publishing activities.

PC: P4

For my father, Gene Carl Hartson,
for sharing with me his wonder and curiosity about this beautiful planet.

Contents

Quick Reference Guide 4
Introduction 6

BALEEN WHALES
PAGE 36

Gray Whales 38

Rorquals 42

Right Whales 58

TOOTHED WHALES
PAGE 64

Belugas 66

Ocean Dolphins 70

Porpoises 92

Beaked Whales 100

Dwarf Sperm Whales 108

Sperm Whales 110

SEALS & OTTERS
PAGE 114

Eared Seals 116

Walruses 124

Hair Seals 128

Otters 148

Glossary 154
Whale Research, Conservation Groups and Further Reading ..156
Index 159

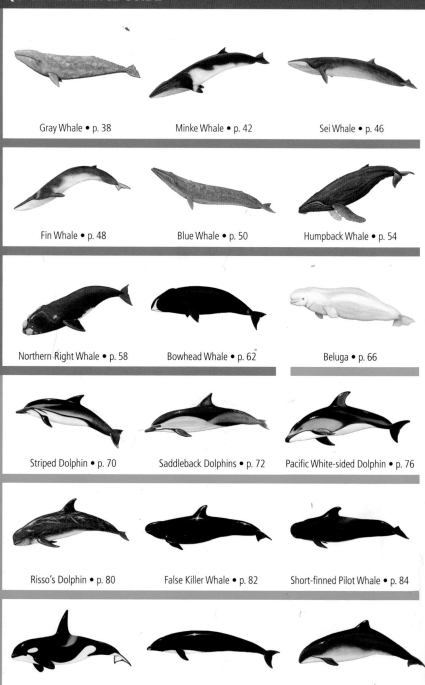

BALEEN WHALES

Gray Whale • p. 38

Minke Whale • p. 42

Sei Whale • p. 46

Fin Whale • p. 48

Blue Whale • p. 50

Humpback Whale • p. 54

Northern Right Whale • p. 58

Bowhead Whale • p. 62

Beluga • p. 66

TOOTHED WHALES

Striped Dolphin • p. 70

Saddleback Dolphins • p. 72

Pacific White-sided Dolphin • p. 76

Risso's Dolphin • p. 80

False Killer Whale • p. 82

Short-finned Pilot Whale • p. 84

Orca • p. 86

Northern Right Whale Dolphin • p. 90

Harbor Porpoise • p. 92

Dall's Porpoise • p. 96

Baird's Beaked Whale • p. 100

Cuvier's Beaked Whale • p. 102

Hubbs's Beaked Whale • p. 104

Stejneger's Beaked Whale • p. 106

Dwarf Sperm Whale • p. 108

Sperm Whale • p. 110

Northern Fur Seal • p. 116

Northern Sea-Lion • p. 118

California Sea-Lion • p. 122

Walrus • p. 124

Harbor Seal • p. 128

Spotted Seal • p. 132

Ringed Seal • p. 134

Ribbon Seal • p. 138

Bearded Seal • p. 140

Northern Elephant Seal • p. 144

Sea Otter • p. 148

Northern River Otter • p. 152

Introduction

In 1969, we saw Earth from the moon. During the first moon landing, pictures of our planet were radioed back to Earth for everyone to see. These first images of Earth kindled a new kind of enlightenment and shifted our awareness of ourselves and our place on the planet. Seeing images of "Spaceship Earth" sparked two (among many) profound realizations that not only affected our thinking at the time, but would eventually affect the relationship between humans and whales. Primarily, the images reminded us that Earth is dominated by oceans. More than 70 percent of our planet's surface is covered by water, and the creatures that thrive in the marine habitat are marvelous in their form and adaptation. The second realization, rather less obvious, is that we may not be alone in this universe, and we conjured up a keen anticipation of finding non-human intelligence. One result of these combined realizations was a new appreciation for those animals that live in the sea, and when we looked into the eyes of whales and saw something familiar and hopefully intelligent, we redoubled our efforts to understand and protect these great creatures.

Whales have fascinated people for thousands of years. At least 3500 years ago, the early Greeks used images of dolphins on mosaics, frescos, vases and coins. Aristotle is believed to be the first person to propose that whales and dolphins are mammals, not fish, and he correctly identified and classified several different species.

When people speak of whales, they generally imagine the large whales that live in deep oceans. Broadly speaking, the distinction between whales, dolphins and porpoises is based on size rather than zoological affinity: whales are typically the largest of the three; porpoises are the smallest. Some of the largest dolphins are larger than the smallest whales, however, so the terminology can be confusing. Technically, whales include the Gray Whale, rorquals, Bowhead Whale, right whales, Beluga, Narwhal, sperm whales and beaked whales. Dolphins include the Orca, pilot whales, ocean dolphins and river dolphins. Many people call the Orca the Killer Whale, but it is really the largest member of the dolphin family. There are only six species of porpoises worldwide.

All whales, dolphins and porpoises are members of the order Cetacea, and they are commonly called "cetaceans." They are distinguished from other mammals by their nearly hairless bodies, paddle-like forelimbs, lack of hindlimbs, fusiform bodies and powerful tail flukes. At least 81 species of cetaceans are known to exist today, and they are scientifically classified into two suborders according to whether they have baleen or teeth. The baleen whales are in the suborder Mysticeti and the toothed whales are in the suborder Odontoceti. There are only 11 species of baleen whales worldwide. They are the rorqual whales, Gray Whale, Bowhead Whale and right whales. There are at least 70 species of toothed whales worldwide, including porpoises, dolphins, sperm whales, the Narwhal, the Beluga and beaked whales.

About This Guide

No matter where it is you are learning about whales, whether aboard a whale-watching boat on the ocean or in the comfort of your own home, keep this book handy for quick reference about whales and other marine mammals. All the species you might encounter off the coasts of British Columbia and Alaska are illustrated and described within this book. As well, historical and biological information is presented to give you a better understanding about whales in general.

About 26 whale species occur in the waters off British Columbia and Alaska. Of these, 8 are baleen whales (mysticetes) and 18 are toothed whales (odontocetes). The most famous and commonly seen cetaceans in this region are the Gray Whale, Humpback Whale, Orca and Harbor Porpoise, but less common cetaceans may be encountered at any time.

The whales of British Columbia and Alaska are presented here in a generally accepted sequence that places the more closely related whales near one another. The scientific names and the ordering of the groups (genera) and species follow the "Revised checklist of North American mammals north of Mexico, 1997" (Occasional Paper No. 173, Museum of Texas Tech University, by Jones, Hoffmann, Rice et al. 1997). The section describing the other marine mammals in the region is similarly ordered, but placed after the section on whales. The common names used in this book are widely accepted and frequently used names. However, owing to discrepancies in the common names of many species, some species may be found under different names in other texts. Wherever necessary, the alternate common names are included in each entry as well as in the index.

The quick reference guide on pages 4 and 5 illustrates all the species in the book. It may help you identify species and groups at a glance, and it leads you to the detailed descriptions of each species. The blows and dive sequences for selected species are also illustrated together on pages 20 and 21. The glossary (pp. 154–55) defines some of the specialized terms that are used in talking about whales, and it also includes labeled diagrams of the main cetacean bodyparts.

Each species account includes a "Status" entry, giving information on the current conservation status of the species. Descriptions such as "endangered," "threatened" and "vulnerable" are official designations made either by the U.S. Fish and Wildlife Service (USFWS) or the Committee on the Status of Endangered Wildlife in Canada (COSEWIC) and are defined in the glossary. Other descriptions appearing in the book, such as "common," "stable" or "declining," are used in accordance with current local research.

It should be noted that the lifecycles of many whales are described in terms of the animal's size, instead of its age. Because of our limited understanding of cetaceans, we are unable to estimate an individual's age for most species, whereas length can be readily measured in the field.

Because some whales are so very large, it can be hard to get a good visual idea of their size. To help you with this task, below the size measurements, we show a scaled comparison between an average-sized individual of each species and either a human diver (about 6 ft [1.8 m] long) or a school bus (about 35 ft [11 m] long).

The "Similar Species" section in each species account lists other whales or marine mammals that could easily be confused with the whale you are reading about. Be sure to check these other species before you decide on the identity of a whale in the wild.

Once you have learned to identify whales and you are familiar with their natural history, enjoy them! Whales are marvelous creatures and watching them can be a thrilling and memorable experience.

Whale Watching on the West Coast

Whale watching has become a worldwide activity that attracts millions of people each year. The coasts of British Columbia and Alaska have many famous sites where whale watchers can easily see Orcas and Gray, Humpback and Minke whales. Other species that can be seen unexpectedly at any time are Blue, Fin, Sei and Sperm whales. As for smaller species, Pacific White-sided Dolphins and Dall's and Harbor porpoises can be seen in certain locations. The preceding species are the most frequently seen whales, but remember that every species in this book can be found in the waters of British Columbia or Alaska. Keep your eyes open for the rarer whales—positive sightings are worth reporting to local research stations.

The west coast of North America has some of the most exciting places in the world for viewing and studying whales. Despite past whaling and current heavy boat traffic, the fjords, straits, sounds and food-rich waters of our coast form prime habitat for many species of whales. Gray Whales perform their long migration along this coast, and some of the best-known and most-studied populations of Orcas and Humpbacks also inhabit these waters.

While it is true that you may encounter whales throughout the coastal region of British Columbia and Alaska, some places are better than others to find whales. The map on the facing page illustrates the best sites for whale watching, which also correlates to good availability of whale-watching tours. With respect, the places where whales are sensitive to disturbance or places that are ecologically fragile have not been included. Nevertheless, some of the best whale-watching sites in the world are here, ready for you to explore.

The B.C. portion of the North Pacific coast alone is 17,000 mi (27,000 km) in length. This great length is attributable to the complex network of islands, inlets, fjords and estuaries. The resulting sheltered water is preferred by several whale species. Water characteristics and availability of food is also an important factor determining whale density. The North Pacific Current causes upwellings of cold, nutrient-rich water from the deep ocean bottom. Animal and plant life is abundant because of this upwelling, and many

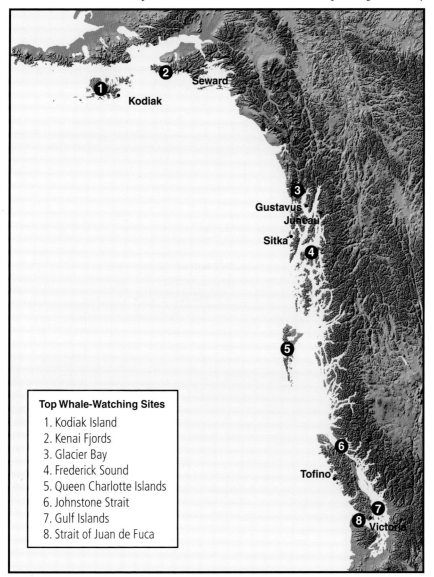

Top Whale-Watching Sites
1. Kodiak Island
2. Kenai Fjords
3. Glacier Bay
4. Frederick Sound
5. Queen Charlotte Islands
6. Johnstone Strait
7. Gulf Islands
8. Strait of Juan de Fuca

species of animals grow larger here than their relatives do in less-rich water elsewhere. Planktonic invertebrates are extremely abundant, and these feed the large baleen whales. Fish are also abundant in the cold water, and they become food for the toothed whales, seals and sea-lions.

There are many choices to make if you are to have a successful whale-watching adventure. The time of year is important: catching the peak of migration makes for the best chances of seeing certain species. Some species, such as Orcas, can be seen year-round, although they are much less common in winter. If you want to take a boat tour, you can choose between a day trip or a multiple-day cruise. Costs vary depending on how long a trip you are taking.

Always research who is operating the tour. A tour leader should be knowledgeable of whale biology and up to date on current locations of different whales. It is essential that the tour operator is responsible and behaves ethically around whales. Like people, whales have personalities and personal space requirements, and boaters that harass whales (even unknowingly) can be extremely disruptive to the animal and can cause unnecessary stress and harm. In the worst cases, a whale that is badly harassed may show aggression towards boaters and can suffer stress or injuries. In the best cases, a whale may be comfortable with your presence and approach your boat on its own accord to get a better look at you. If you are the skipper of your own boat, know the basic guidelines for approaching whales. The most stringent and concise rules on the West Coast are those from Alaska:

• Minimum approach distance is 300 ft (91 m).
• Approach or leave whales at "no-wake" speed from the side or behind (never from ahead) with no sudden changes in speed or direction.
• If a whale approaches, put the engine in neutral and allow it to pass.
• Never follow whales or herd, drive or separate them, particularly mothers and calves.
• Only one vessel at a time at the minimum approach distance.
• There is a time limit of 30 minutes per vessel at the minimum distance.
• Swimmers should not approach within 150 ft (46 m).

The U.S. Marine Mammal Protection Act of 1972 prohibits the harassing, capturing or killing of any marine mammal. Anyone breaking this law is subject to fines of up to US$25,000 or imprisonment. Most tour operators are knowledgeable, responsible and show genuine concern for the welfare of whales. If you encounter people who are not following proper conduct around whales, please speak up. Let them know they are interfering with and possibly harming the whales. If everyone acts responsibly, the whales will probably stay in the vicinity for everyone to enjoy.

The industry of whale watching is more than just the intrinsic pleasure of seeing these great creatures. On the West Coast, from Alaska to Oregon, whale watching brings in at least $5 million each year. The accessory items related to whale watching are an additional $2 million to $3 million, at least. To look at whale watching in monetary terms is important if whale conservation is to be politically and economically acceptable. On the other hand, attaching dollar figures to whale watching is superficial at best. How can we put a dollar figure on awe-inspiring experiences in the wild? As every whale watcher knows, the true value is in the extraordinary and breathtaking encounter with a wild whale.

Whale Origins and Evolution

The evolutionary history of whales is truly remarkable. Mammals originated on land, so cetaceans must have arisen from terrestrial ancestors. In fact, their closest living relatives are the artiodactyls: even-toed hoofed mammals such as cattle, antelopes, pigs and hippopotamuses. The artiodactyls and the cetaceans have common ancestors that are unlike either of these present-day groups.

Mammals existed as early as 210 million years ago, but the great dinosaurs dominated the world until 65 million years ago, and mammals remained very small and insignificant. After the dinosaurs died out, mammals had the chance to diversify, and they evolved to walk the earth, fly in the sky and swim in the oceans. The first ancestor of whales known through fossil finds is likely 50-million-year-old Ambulocetus, an amphibious, dolphin-sized mammal that had hindlegs with webbed feet for swimming. Ambulocetus probably gave rise to Pakicetus, which still had legs, but had a more whale-like skull, teeth, jaw and tail stock. By the early Oligocene (34 million years ago) several toothed whales existed, and Mammalodon, the baleen whale ancestor, also appeared. Once the basic physiology was established, cetaceans diversified dramatically, and by about 7 million years ago, the major forms of whales, dolphins and porpoises that we recognize today had evolved.

Pakicetus

Over millions of years of evolution, the body plan of the whale changed dramatically from a four-legged progenitor to the streamlined oceanic form we see today. The loss of the hindlimbs and the modification of the forelimbs into flippers with no moving elbows are striking changes to the basic mammalian plan. Whales still retain a vestigial pelvis and femur, because selective pressure for eliminating such structures is weak. The blowhole originated from the nostrils, which migrated to the top of the head and effectively separated breathing and eating. The ears were modified for hearing underwater, and echolocation developed in the toothed whales. The dorsal line of the whale adapted to create better propulsion underwater: the neck vertebrae stiffened, a dorsal fin originated, muscles and bones along the tail stock strengthened, and the tail flukes developed. Skulls and jaws were highly modified, and about 33 to 34 million years ago, the division between baleen and toothed whales occurred. This division was paramount, because the baleen whales became specialized for catching large quantities of small creatures, while the toothed whales could catch smaller quantities of larger prey. Other modified features include a highly streamlined body and a nearly total loss of body hair.

Although whales and dolphins evolved in the oceans, some species now live in fresh water. The river dolphins, which number five species worldwide, inhabit large river systems, such as the Amazon, Orinoco, Indus, Ganges and Yangtze. As well, most porpoises can travel freely between fresh and salt water, as can the Beluga. Generally speaking, however, the saltwater whales tire quickly in fresh water (because of their reduced buoyancy), and their skin might wrinkle and slough (just like ours does in a bath).

The fact that whales look a bit like sharks is a tribute to convergent evolution. Sharks and whales are not closely related at all, and there are many physiological differences between them, but their similar appearance reflects a desirable body plan for being a successful ocean creature. A gray-colored shark and a dolphin, for example, may be difficult to distinguish at first glance.

Shark

Dolphin

Although mammals have many characteristics that differentiate them from other animals, the most obvious differences between whales and sharks are that whales breathe air and nurse their young, while sharks have gills and do not nurse their young. The easiest way to distinguish between sharks and whales, however, is to look at their tails: the flukes of a cetacean are horizontal; the tail of a shark is vertical. Many frightened swimmers have thought an approaching dolphin was a shark, but a shark swimming close to the surface of the water reveals two triangular "fins" above the surface: its dorsal fin and the top of its tail. Dolphins, on the other hand, only reveal their dorsal fin.

Behavior and Adaptations

FEEDING WITH BALEEN

The baleen whales, or mysticetes, are typically the largest of all cetaceans. Of these, the largest are the females. Ironically, these large whales feed on some of the tiniest ocean creatures.

Baleen specialized for skim-feeding
(Bowhead Whale)

Baleen specialized for lunge-feeding
(Minke Whale)

Baleen plates are a remarkable new mammalian adaptation that permits efficient filter-feeding of plankton, tiny crustaceans, small fish and some mollusks from the ocean water. Baleen was once called "whalebone," but it is really not bone at all. Although baleen grows where teeth normally would on other mammals, it is actually made of an entirely different keratinous material very similar to human fingernails and hair. The baleen plates grow down from the gum of the upper jaw, and they are shaped like very long, narrow triangles. All the plates hang one against the other, similar to vertical blinds on a livingroom window. The hairs on the edge of each plate face into the mouth.

Lunge-feeding, also known as gulp-feeding, and skim-feeding are the two basic styles of feeding among baleen whales. Within each style, there is variation between species and even individuals.

The rorqual whales primarily use lunge-feeding. If necessary, prior to lunging, the whale herds its prey into a tight group near the surface. Once the prey is concentrated, the whale lunges and opens its mouth to gulp in tons of food-rich water. A rorqual has

Throat distension during lunge-feeding

specialized throat pleats that expand like an accordion and allow the throat to distend to balloon-like dimensions. These pleats contract automatically as the whale closes its gaping mouth. The mouth is not closed completely, but just enough to permit the baleen to meet the lower jaw and create a sieve. The water is squeezed out through the baleen, while the krill, copepods and other small creatures are trapped inside the mouth against the baleen. Rorquals have short baleen that is continuous around the front of the jaw, making the mouth an effective filter when it is nearly closed.

A famous variation of lunge-feeding is when Humpback Whales use bubble-netting. One or several Humpbacks begin releasing bubbles as they swim in a circle below a school of fish. As the bubbles rise, they create a curtain that disorients the fish and traps them in a central area. Once the fish are concentrated inside this bubble-net, the whales surge up in the middle of the "net" and gulp the creatures into their gaping mouths.

Skim-feeding is passive by comparison to lunge-feeding, and it is a style utilized primarily by right whales and the Bowhead Whale. The Sei Whale, although it is a rorqual, frequently uses

Humpback Whale bubble-netting

skim-feeding, as well. For a long time, skim-feeding was believed to occur at or near the surface, simply because we could see the whales doing it there. Skim-feeding often occurs at great depths, however, and only recently was this activity recorded on film by researchers.

This feeding style requires the whale to swim through a school of plankton or other small creatures with its mouth open.

Bowhead and right whales do not have baleen in the front of their mouths, and the baleen on the sides is very long. When the whale opens its mouth, the opening is like a small cave with walls of baleen. As the whale swims through the food-rich water, the water enters the mouth and continues right out through the baleen. Food also goes into the mouth, but it is trapped by the long baleen. The throats of these whales do not extend, and the mouth is kept still and open as the whale swims. Once many food creatures have accumulated in the mouth, the whale closes its jaws and swallows.

Northern Right Whale skim-feeding

FEEDING WITH TEETH

The toothed whales feed on creatures larger than those fed on by baleen whales. Their jaws are modified depending on their style of feeding and their prey. Dolphins, for example, often have long, narrow jaws that are fast-closing and capable of catching small, darting fish. Orcas, on the other hand, have wider jaws with heavy, conical teeth for holding prey and tearing off large chunks. The size of its prey matters little to the Orca, and certain groups of Orcas are known to regularly attack other cetaceans, such as porpoises, dolphins and even larger whales, especially sick or injured ones. Porpoises have spade-shaped teeth that are flattened side to side. These teeth are effective for slicing and shearing, rather than holding prey.

Orca teeth

Dolphin teeth

The Sperm Whale and the beaked whales are believed to be suction feeders—by quickly moving the tongue backward in the mouth, they create a powerful suction to pull in their prey—and there is much debate about how useful teeth are to them. The Sperm Whale has a very narrow jaw, relative to the size of its head, with heavy, conical teeth. The white mouth of the Sperm Whale may even act like a lure to bring its prey close. One adult Sperm Whale that was killed had no lower jaw at all—an astonishing injury that appeared to have little effect on the overall health of the whale, which was large and clearly well-fed.

Beaked whales have some of the strangest teeth and jaws of all the odontocetes. Usually, only the male's teeth erupt, while the females feed without any functional teeth. Males have two teeth (sometimes four) in the lower jaw, either close to the tip of the beak or in the middle. The teeth tend to be large and triangular shaped, and sometimes they overlap the upper jaw on the outside of the mouth.

THE BLOWHOLE

Single blowhole of toothed whales

Paired blowholes of baleen whales

One of the marvels of cetacean anatomy is the blowhole. Unable to breathe through its mouth, a whale inhales and exhales exclusively through its blowhole. The blowhole is designed for rapid air exchange, and it is the result of an evolutionary change in skull shape and a slow migration of the nostrils and breathing passage to the top of the head—away from the throat. In some cases, most notably the Humpback Whale, air can voluntarily be released from the lungs into the mouth if the trachea is slightly dislodged, but this action does not give the whale the ability to breathe through its mouth.

For whales, breathing is voluntary, and they open and close their blowholes at will. The baleen whales have two blowholes that are controlled by strong muscles attached to the upper jaw. When they surface, they make an explosive blow and inhale in such quick succession that the entire process takes only a few seconds. The toothed whales appear to have only one blowhole. In fact, they have two nasal passages, each

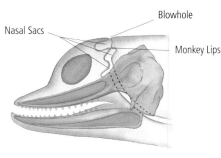

Nasal Sacs

Blowhole

Monkey Lips

with the ability to open and close, but these passages are hidden internally and called "monkey lips." The single, external blowhole is a new adaptation unique to odontocetes that allows for sound generation by the hidden soft tissues of the nasal passages.

SLEEP

Unlike terrestrial mammals, cetaceans do not enter a deep state of sleep. They must rest, but they require much less sleep than terrestrial mammals. Evidence suggests that whales require less sleep because the marine environment induces a brain state that resembles sleep. Even humans, when in water for prolonged periods, may require only one hour of sleep a day where they otherwise would sleep eight hours. Moreover, whales are voluntary breathers, and in order for them to breathe at the surface, to keep moving to prevent stranding and to watch for potential dangers, the whales must never fall soundly asleep. Dolphins and porpoises are able to "sleep" half their brain at a time.

To relax, many whales use the technique of "logging" at the surface. Logging is a form of rest where one or more whales float almost motionless at the surface, all pointing the same direction. Their breathing and heart rates are lowered, and their eyes may close, but they have not totally lost consciousness. Mariners once believed that a logging whale was fast asleep and even an approaching boat could not wake it, but the opposite is true.

LUNGS AND DIVING

Perhaps the greatest danger for a deep-diving air breather is nitrogen narcosis, a desensitized state caused from pressurized air entering the circulation system. The other hazard is called the bends, where bubbles spontaneously form in joints and tissues from rising to the surface too fast. Whales are not affected by either of these conditions because of several adaptations that evolved over time.

Before a deep dive, whales remove the air from their lungs. Air is highly compressible, whereas water is not. Like our bodies, most of a whale's body is water and can therefore handle the pressure of a dive. Only the air in the lungs is subject to compression. Any air that remains in a whale's lungs is pushed into the inflexible windpipe where it cannot be compressed. This

Sperm Whale diving

strategy prevents air compression and thereby effectively eliminates nitrogen narcosis. The bends, also known as decompression sickness, is prevented by the efficient and rapid transport of nitrogen back into the lungs as the whale surfaces. Circulation of blood through the muscles during the dive is also reduced, which further reduces the possibility of bubbles of nitrogen forming.

SOUNDS AND SONGS

In water, sound travels almost five times faster than in air. A cetacean uses sound to keep in touch with other members of its group, and some of the odontocetes use sound for echolocation. Different whales make different sounds, and if the sounds have meaning, one species likely cannot understand those of another species. Sounds vary from loud to quiet, and from deep rumbles and belches to high squeaks and clicks.

Baleen whales commonly produce the deepest and loudest sounds. The vocalizations of a Blue Whale can be less than 20 hertz in frequency and up to 188 decibels in volume. Sophisticated military technology capable of detecting submarine sounds from far away has been able to pick up the sounds of a Blue Whale from over 1500 mi (2400 km) away.

This kind of evidence changes how we look at a group of whales. Perhaps whales do not have to be in visual range to be considered part of the same group. Two rorqual whales seen 30 mi (48 km) apart may not be "solo" whales. Humpback Whales make extremely loud and long songs. Samples of the unique and complex songs of Humpbacks have even been sent out on Voyagers 1 and 2, spacecraft that are on their way toward other worlds in this galaxy. This sample of Humpback song is in a section of recording that includes greetings in 55 languages from 60 different countries.

Although Humpbacks are now part of the ambassadorial elite of Earth, no one actually knows how they and other baleen whales produce sound. Baleen whales have a larynx, but they have no vocal cords and their paired blowholes release no bubbles when they sing. A laryngeal source for the sound is not ruled out, but much more research must be done to determine how mysticete whales make sound.

In toothed whales, sound production is complex, but it is better understood than sound production in mysticetes. The external blowhole of the toothed whale hides the "monkey lips," or the internal soft tissue of the dual inner nasal passages. The monkey lips can pass air to generate sound, much like we can purse our lips to making squeaking and kissing sounds. One "monkey lip" can be open while the other is closed, creating a variety of different sounds. All the while, the external blowhole stays shut, so no air is released. The sounds made by odontocetes are primarily whistles, squeaks and clicks emitted in a variety of patterns.

Many groups of toothed whales have unique "dialects" different from other groups. All Orcas, for example, produce many similar sounds that are probably understandable from one whale to the next, but closer analysis reveals that one group will produce sound combinations that no other group does. Dolphins also have very sophisticated sounds and sound patterns. Many species have "signature whistles" for each individual, which are probably like human names. Signature whistles are often accompanied by a small string of bubbles released from the blowhole.

ECHOLOCATION

The use of echolocation, while it is rare in the animal kingdom, is not unique to whales. Bats and certain birds are also efficient echolocators, and there may be other animals that use echolocation that we are not aware of yet. Echolocation involves sending out high-frequency pulses or clicks and listening to how these sounds bounce off objects present in the vicinity.

Echolocation, particularly the underwater variety, is also known as sonar (*so*und *na*vigation and *r*anging). Military organizations once applauded themselves for discovering and using such "advanced" technology. Some of this military pride was shattered upon learning that bats and whales had been doing it for millennia.

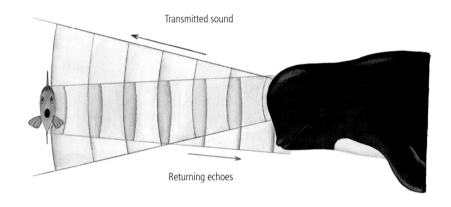

Transmitted sound

Returning echoes

As far as we know, only the odontocetes use echolocation. Some species, such as spotted dolphins, may even use such intense pulses that their prey is momentarily stunned, making feeding much easier.

When toothed whales emit the echolocation clicks, the sounds are passed through the melon—a specialized structure in their foreheads that focuses the sound. The melon is mainly low-density oil, and it gives toothed whales their distinctive, bulbous foreheads. When the outgoing signals hit an object, they bounce back in an altered form. These returning "echoes" are so detailed that the whale can perceive shape, size, texture, distance and probably many more features. The returning signals are received through the lower jaw, which helps transmit the sound to the modified ear.

Echolocation is not limited to surfaces. Evidence indicates that odontocetes can "see" inside things, even inside other bodies, to learn which females (human, dolphin or otherwise) are pregnant. Many interesting research projects involve dolphins and pregnant women, because the dolphins seem to be aware of the pregnancy and act differently around these women. The primary use for echolocation in whales, however, is for finding food and determining the immediate surroundings. The pulses are effective for at least 2500 ft (760 m), and they allow the whales to hunt even in totally dark or murky water.

MIGRATION
Both mysticete and odontocete whales may perform migrations of some sort. The baleen whales typically make long migrations between their feeding waters and their calving and mating waters. Most toothed whales, on the other hand, are more appropriately called

nomadic, because their journeys follow food cycles rather than predetermined paths for certain activities. Sperm Whales, Bottlenosed Whales and Long-finned Pilot Whales make seasonal migrations, but in general, very little is known about toothed whale migrations.

In general, and in both hemispheres, baleen whales migrate from high-latitude feeding waters to low-latitude calving and mating waters. The whales often feed only in the high-latitude waters, and during periods of calving, mating and migrating, they consume little or no food. The foods that baleen whales feed on—primarily plankton, krill, copepods and small fish—are particularly abundant in the high-latitude waters. Some theories suggest the baleen whales migrate to warm waters each year because their calves may not be able to survive in the cold, food-rich water, but there is little evidence to support such claims.

The details of why whales migrate may forever remain a mystery to us, as may the mechanics of how they unerringly traverse thousand of miles of water. The long swim of a migrating baleen whale takes two or three months in each direction. It travels nearly constantly at speeds of just a few miles an hour. The cues a whale uses to navigate are not well understood. Perhaps it spy-hops occasionally to follow natural coastal features, or it may be able to detect subtle changes in water "tastes" and currents. Some researchers suggest that whales can use the sun and stars as a compass like we do, or they may be able to follow seafloor topography. Some cetaceans have the mineral magnetite (iron oxide) present in their bodies, and this is a key substance for biomagnetism. (Biomagnetism is when an animal can orient itself to the magnetic field of the Earth, and perhaps use this ability for traveling long distances.) Whichever way they do it, whales continue to dazzle the researchers with their ability to travel and properly navigate over long distances.

STRANDINGS

Strandings are staggering events where whales end up in shallow water and can no longer maneuver. If the tide goes out, the whale is left dry on the sand, where it usually dies. Stranding can happen to one whale or to hundreds of whales at a time.

No one seems to know why some cetaceans become stranded. Some people think that in areas of gently sloping beaches, the echolocation of the odontocete whales is distorted. It is true that strandings occur more often with deep-water species, such as Sperm Whales or pilot whales, as if they become disoriented if they get too close to the coastline. Cetaceans that regularly live in coastal waters, such as dolphins and porpoises, rarely strand. In these cases, the individuals that strand are usually injured or diseased. Beluga Whales may strand when high numbers of them congregate into estuaries and shallow bays. As long as a Polar Bear does not find it, a stranded Beluga will live until the next tide comes to free it.

In situations where whales are found alive and stranded, do not attempt to touch them or help them. In some countries, it is illegal to help whales unless you have proper training. Unskilled "help" for a stranded whale has often resulted in greater harm to the whale and injuries to the person. The first thing to do in the event of a stranding is contact the nearest wildlife authorities or the police. If necessary, the immediate first aid for a stranded whale is to make sure its blowhole is unobstructed by sand or debris so it can breathe, and to keep its skin moist so it does not get sunburned or dehydrated.

DISPLAYS AND SURFACE BEHAVIOR

BREACHING: This behavior is a favorite for whale watchers. A breach is when some or all of the whale's body rises out of the water and splashes back in. Why whales breach is not clear. They may enjoy it, it may help rid the body of barnacles and parasites, or they may do it if they feel insecure or threatened. In some cases, whales breach repeatedly, much to the delight and astonishment of nearby whale watchers. Although many people assume that such instances are positive for both the people and the whale, some researchers suspect that the whale is breaching due to distress from boat harassment. Dolphins may breach in a high leap clear out of the water and spin or somersault while in the air.

LOB-TAILING: The lob-tail is when a whale forcefully slaps its flukes on the surface of the water while its upper body remains submerged. When a whale lob-tails, it can be interpreted in many ways. Some species are known to lob-tail as a sign of aggression, while others appear to do it for much more benign reasons, such as communication.

SPY-HOPPING: Most whales engage in spy-hopping, especially while traveling. Spy-hopping is when a whale raises its head almost vertically out of the water as if to get a better look around. This may be exactly what it is doing, because whales typically only rise until their eyes are exposed and no more.

FLIPPER-SLAPPING: Cetaceans may occasionally roll on to one side and slap their flippers against the surface of the water. This behavior may be repeated several times in a row, but we do not understand what it signifies.

FLUKING: Before a whale dives, it frequently raises its flukes above the surface of the water. For many species, this action indicates that a long, deep dive has started. Many researchers use the markings and scars on the flukes of whales to identify and catalogue individuals.

LOGGING: For most species, one to several whales may "log" at the surface as a form of rest. When several individuals log, they all face the same direction and stay in a close group. Logging requires minimal effort, but is not an unconscious state, because the whale must remain at least semi-conscious at all times in order to breathe.

BOW-RIDING: Dolphins, porpoises and some small whales frequently engage in bow-riding and wake-riding. Dolphins appear to enjoy this activity, and people certainly enjoy watching them. The pressure wave created from a moving boat pushes the dolphins along at great speeds with minimal energy output by the animal.

RUBBING: Rubbing is a behavior done by several species and is probably to massage the skin, aid in molting or simply to feel good. Orcas massage themselves on shallow underwater beaches of rounded pebbles, which in some cases is visible to a boater above. Belugas molt annually, and they gather in shallow bays where they rub themselves to quicken the process.

PLAYING: Probably all cetaceans engage in playing activity. Play can be anything, and may involve juveniles learning particular behaviors that will aid them as adults. If you see whales or dolphins playing at the surface, enjoy watching them, but try not to disturb their fun or harass them.

BLOWING: One of the first indications that a whale is nearby is the distinct blow it makes upon surfacing. The blow of a whale is probably visible because of a combination of factors. The difference in temperature between the whale's lungs and the outside air, some seawater from the skin's surface and accumulated droplets of mucus and oils from the whale's lungs and nasal passages probably all contribute to the blow. The shape and size of the blow varies between species. Some species, such as the Sperm Whale, have such unique blows that seeing the blow alone can identify the whale. Within a species, blow shape and size also vary. Typically, the first blow after a long dive is louder and bigger than proceeding blows. Blows may be diagnostic of the species when viewed from the front or rear. Side views may not be as distinct. The blows illustrated on the following pages are to scale and are all viewed from the front.

DIVE SEQUENCE: The most frequently observed activity at the surface is the dive sequence. Beginning with a blow, the dive sequence reveals certain characteristics about the animal. The shape of the head and blowhole, the length of the back, the dorsal fin, any dorsal knuckles or bumps, the tail stock and the flukes are all features that may be seen in a dive and that are diagnostic enough to identify the species.

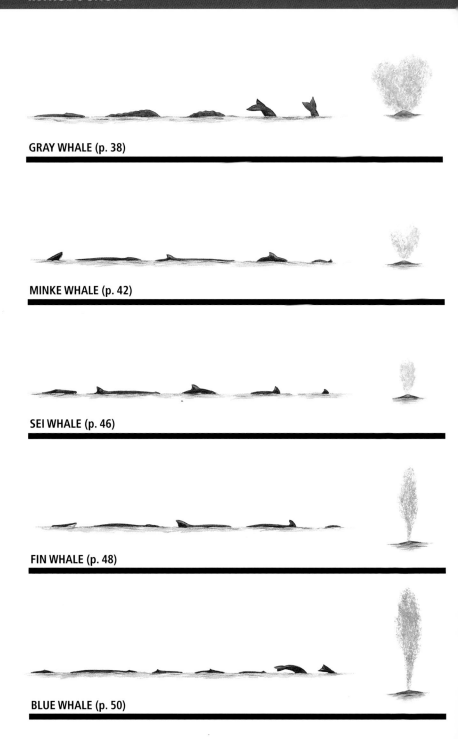

GRAY WHALE (p. 38)

MINKE WHALE (p. 42)

SEI WHALE (p. 46)

FIN WHALE (p. 48)

BLUE WHALE (p. 50)

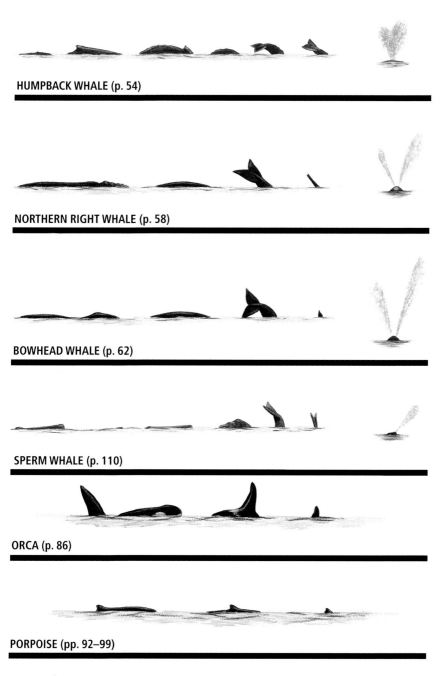

HUMPBACK WHALE (p. 54)

NORTHERN RIGHT WHALE (p. 58)

BOWHEAD WHALE (p. 62)

SPERM WHALE (p. 110)

ORCA (p. 86)

PORPOISE (pp. 92–99)

Intelligence and Whale Research

A common question people ask is "How intelligent are whales?" To answer this honestly, we do not know. Many studies have been done with whales to determine their intellectual abilities, but we do not have accurate ways of measuring intelligence in animals other than humans. Also, whales, dolphins and porpoises differ in intelligence amongst themselves. For example, most people would agree that Orcas and Bottlenosed Dolphins are more intelligent than river dolphins. Even how we define intelligence is ambiguous: it can mean independent thinking, analytical skills, understanding and evaluation skills or the ability to use reason and judgment in daily life. Intelligence can also be measured as a correlation between brain size and brain complexity.

Another difficulty arises in how we test cetacean intelligence. We require whales and dolphins to learn our signals and sounds, and then complete performance and ability tests. The inherent flaw in these procedures is that we are not measuring how intelligent a whale is with such tests, we are only learning how well they do on tests designed by us. By learning the sounds, signals and performance abilities of whales and dolphins in their own environment, we may learn far more about the intelligence of these creatures.

Looking at the brain of a cetacean is an indication of its potential intelligence. Unfortunately, the ratio of body size to brain size (also called the encephalization quotient) does not directly correlate with intelligence level. Bottlenosed Dolphins have larger brains than humans in absolute terms, but their encephalization quotient is smaller. Bottlenosed Dolphins and Chimpanzees have a similar encephalization quotient. The complexity of a Bottlenosed Dolphin's brain is high, however, and it has well-developed cerebral cortices (the part of the brain associated with learning and abstract thought). Some people argue that this level of complexity serves to coordinate their motor processes and echolocation, rather than being a sign of true intelligence.

Problem solving and the ability to learn are two well-accepted ways to assess intelligence. Whales in the wild show signs of teaching each other new things they have learned, and certainly mothers teach their calves many techniques for living. In captivity, cetaceans learn complex routines very quickly, and they even learn our language symbols. Studies with Bottlenosed Dolphins indicate they understand some abstract concepts like "sameness" and "difference." Using sign language, a dolphin easily understands the difference between "take the ball to the hoop" and "take the hoop to the ball." Dolphins seem quite capable of learning the basics of our language and signals, but we have still a long way to go to learn their sounds and language. (Researchers debate about definitions of language, and whether or not cetaceans have true language. Nevertheless, it is clear to any observer that dolphins use sounds between one another and these sounds appear to have intention and even meaning.)

Some dolphins and whales appear to have good levels of problem solving, and there are several well-known examples of problem solving in wild cetaceans. In the wild, Bottlenosed Dolphins have been observed using tools in problem situations, such as wielding the spines from a dead, poisonous fish to oust an eel from its crevice. Many researchers believe that the cooperative bubble-netting demonstrated by Humpback Whales is an intentional act of cooperation to solve a common problem, although other researchers feel this behavior may be simply instinctive. During heavy whaling years two centuries ago, Sperm Whales were frequently reported to swim and dive in directions upwind when pursued by a sailing vessel. Because sailing vessels cannot travel directly upwind, this behavior could indicate a high level of reasoning or problem solving ability in Sperm Whales, as well as an awareness of the consequences of being caught.

The difficulty with problem solving studies is to differentiate between instinctual responses and actual judgment and evaluation. Problem solving and behavioral studies are excellent forms of research that continually lead to a greater understanding of cetacean ability.

In British Columbia and neighboring regions, whale research in the wild is becoming much more sophisticated. Satellite transmitters are being attached to many species to better understand their migration patterns. Photographic catalogues are used to identify hundreds of individual whales of many different species, especially Orcas and Humpback Whales. Orcas are reliably identified by the shape and scarring of their dorsal fins and by the shape and coloration of the "saddle" patch directly behind the dorsal fin. Humpback Whales can be recognized by the undersides of their tail flukes. The fluke coloration, shape and scarring patterns are used to identify individuals just like fingerprints are used to identify humans. Knowing the individuals means we can follow their movements and record their behaviors.

New diving technology allows divers to breathe underwater without releasing bubbles. Because many whales release bubbles as a threat or when they are alarmed, a diver who releases bubbles likely disturbs the whale and therefore alters its behavior. Since researchers have used this new diving technology, they have been able to observe male Humpbacks as they "sing." With the old kind of scuba gear, the bubbles alerted the whale and it would immediately stop singing. The challenges of studying whales in the wild are great, but as we develop and apply new technology we are able to learn more about the whales and their environment.

Whale Lore:
From Legends to Modern Mythology

For many cultures, whales have been powerful symbols of creation, perfection and even prophecy. Perhaps the earliest depiction of a cetacean is found in Norway, where an ancient carving of an Orca lingers on the coastal rocks and is believed to be about 9000 years old. The ancient Greeks recognized the intelligence and friendliness of dolphins, and they regularly used dolphin motifs in their sculptures, frescos, pottery, coins and paintings. Certain accounts of Greek mythology attach great meaning and spirituality to the dolphin. In one version of creation, all of life originated within a dolphin, hence the Greek species name *delphys*, which means "womb."

On the West Coast, many indigenous peoples included cetaceans in their mythology in some way. Orcas are an important part of First Nations tradition in British Columbia—they are meshed into the social, religious and imaginative life of the people.

A common myth about Orcas that permeates both literature and research is that Orcas have never attacked a human. The Tlingit people of northern British Columbia tell a story of Noht-sy-cla-nay, the man who created the Whale Killer (Killer Whale). Noht-sy-cla-nay created this creature as a favor to the sea-lions, whom he stayed with for a time after his two evil brothers-in-law left him to die on a reef. Months later, after the Whale Killer was created, Noht-sy-cla-nay saw his brothers-in-law in a canoe, and he summoned his Whale Killer to smash the canoe and drown the men inside. After this revenge, Noht-sy-cla-nay said to the Whale Killer, "I made you to kill whales and help the sea-lions, so you must never kill another man again."

Farther north, the Inuit are strongly associated with the Bowhead Whale and the other arctic-dwelling cetaceans. In one Inupiat legend, called "The Gift of the Whale," the Bowhead is portrayed as the final and best creation of the Great Spirit. In this legend, the Great Spirit realizes that the Inupiat people require the Bowhead Whale to live, and he therefore gives the people permission to kill this whale as long as they show respect to the animal and take only what they need to survive. Once a year, in spring, the Inupiat people traditionally kill a small number of Bowhead Whales, and, according to the legend, there is always a heavy fog that hangs in the air above the Inupiat hunters. When the people questioned the Great Spirit about why this cloud occurs, he answered that although he has given them permission to kill his perfect creation, he does not wish to watch it.

In recent centuries, many humans feared whales, and contact with them was limited either to hunting or to occasional events of strandings. Mariners told outlandish stories of attacks by great sea creatures that spouted a toxic substance capable of peeling away your skin and blinding your eyes. Artists engraved terrible scenes of freakish giants capsizing boats and lashing out with their tails. Such perceptions were later replaced by phrases like "gentle giants" and stories of whales and dolphins saving human lives. These stories may be true, but the value and appreciation of cetaceans is not dependent solely on their interaction with humans. Indeed, the truth about whales lies somewhere in-between: they are not quite the gentle and obsequious giants that many people

Orca totem pole

believe them to be, but they are certainly not evil behemoths that lurk beneath our boats ready to strike.

Whale mythology is not limited to the historical perceptions and accounts of these great creatures. Throughout modern literature and arts, whales have been exemplified, celebrated and somewhat idealized. Some famous works include Herman Melville's *Moby Dick*, Hollywood's *Star Trek: The Voyage Home* and *Free Willy*, television's *Flipper* and even Disney's *Pinocchio*. Such stories and films continually add to the rich tradition of whale lore.

Today, the perception and treatment of whales varies considerably between different people of the world. Many people view the whale as a superb opportunity to study mammalian adaptation, while others see the whale as a form of entertainment. Many societies hunt whales for meat and profit; others consider the whale a creature of inherent value outside of human valuation schemes. Regardless of how we look at whales, we share an increasingly intense and intricate relationship with them. Whales, dolphins and porpoises now attract millions of people each year to coastal areas throughout the world. Their special intrigue comes of their intelligence and sheer magnificence. Watching a Humpback Whale breach and fall back into the water with a tremendous splash, or seeing a dolphin's eye turn to look at you as it bow-rides against your boat are extraordinary encounters that leave behind a feeling of contact with very special creatures. Cetaceans demand our respect as powerful creatures that can be very friendly and inquisitive in most circumstances, but rightfully protective and aggressive when they are harassed.

Whales in Peril

UNDERSTANDING WHALING

For centuries, whaling was considered a heroic profession that provided many necessary raw materials for a growing society. While the men were at sea, the needs of the people back on land perpetuated the demand for whale products. A staggering array of goods were made from whale parts, making a list so long and composing so many unexpected products that it is no wonder the whaling industry was lucrative. Whale oil was used in lamps, lipsticks, soaps, shampoos, cooking goods, ice cream, crayons, glycerin for explosives, lotions, machinery lubricants, candles, leather processing, varnishes, adhesives—the list includes virtually everything that requires oil in some way. Baleen from whales has been used for only slightly fewer things, including, but not limited to, umbrella ribs, corsets, whips, window shutters, fishing rods, dress hoops, hairbrushes and shoehorns. Whale meat and blubber was—and still is—eaten by many people; teeth were used as ivory for artworks or piano keys; bones were used for building structures or were ground down to make fertilizer; tendons were used for string and catgut; whale skin could be tanned for leather and the intestinal linings could be stretched and used as transparent window panes. Even ambergris, a hard and waxy digestive by-product that forms in the gut of a Sperm Whale, was used as a fixative for perfumes and once valued at up to $806 a pound. Most people who hunted whales made tremendous effort to utilize every part of the whale and leave nothing to waste. The major difference in usage between groups of people was that some cultures were subsistence whalers and required the whale for their survival, while other cultures were commercial whalers and used the whale for profit.

The evidence of a successful whaling industry is indisputable—millions of whales have been killed over the last two centuries, so many, in fact, that several species may never recover. In the 1940s, when whale populations were at their lowest, no one could deny that if whaling was not dramatically curtailed, there would be no more large whales. From sheer necessity, the International Whaling Commission (IWC) formed in 1948 and began the first management strategy for the industry and the countries involved in whaling. Unfortunately, the quotas and agreements developed by the IWC were never adhered to, and whaling continued. Moreover, for those countries that reported their annual whale takes to the IWC, most figures were as low as 5 percent of the actual number of whales that they killed. Even now, many countries still hunt whales for sustenance, and others still hunt whales for profit.

A strong argument can be made that the small reduction in whaling that occurred up until the early 1990s happened not because of a global effort to save the whales, but because of a combination of two circumstances: primarily, the whale populations were decimated and catches of hundreds of whales each month were no longer possible; secondarily, owing to the evolution of society, our demand for whale products also changed. Electricity greatly reduced the need for whale oil as a lighting agent, and plastics replaced many of the uses for baleen (and corsets, thankfully, went out of fashion).

Explosive harpoon

In view of the large number of uses for whale products, and though it may not be condonable, it is at the very least understandable that the industry heightened to the point of overexploiting the resource. After 1925, the combined effect of explosive harpoons, high-speed whaling vessels and floating whale-processing factories marked the peak of commercial whaling. The catch sizes over the next few decades alone were staggering, especially in the antarctic waters. The Fin Whale, previously too fast for the whaling vessels to catch, took the brunt of the onslaught, and nearly 750,000 were killed. Other large whales were taken as well: more than 360,000 Blue Whales, 200,000 Humpback Whales, 200,000 Sei Whales, nearly 400,000 Sperm Whales and more than 100,000 Minke Whales. These numbers represent just a short period in whaling history when whaling vessels could finally catch the faster whales. In the 1800s, the numbers are equally high for the slower whales, such as the right whales and Bowhead Whale.

Only in the past 10 years has there been a real and obvious reduction in the number of whales killed annually, attributable to the efforts of conservation groups and a worldwide awareness of the plight of whales. Unfortunately, many species are far from safe, and their numbers are far from stable. The Northern Right Whale is undeniably the most endangered large whale on Earth—only a few hundred survive, and most biologists fear it is too late for this species.

WEST COAST WHALING

The history of whaling on the West Coast is long and certainly diverse. The earliest whales hunted were the slow Northern Right, Bowhead and Gray whales. Putting a date on the first whaling event is nearly impossible, because people were known to eat small whales as early as 6000 years ago. Whether these whales were found stranded or were actually hunted is unknown. Almost certainly, First Nations people hunted whales 2000 years ago.

The Nootka (Nuu-chah-nulth) of Vancouver Island and the Inuit of northern Alaska were among the first whalers in the northwest. Nootka whaling was controlled by a chief who had the spiritual power necessary to bring whales close to shore and enough skill and strength to kill them. The Tlingit and Kwakiutl (Kwakwa'ka'wakw) people also hunted whales, and many other groups may have killed whales infrequently. For most aboriginal people, hunting involved pursuing whales in large dugout canoes or smaller kayaks, with spears and harpoons that had either stone or mussel-shell blades.

Killing the whale was only half the battle. Once the whale was dead, the people had to tow its enormous body back to shore behind their comparatively small canoes. The Aleuts of the Aleutian Islands had a different method—they would tip their harpoons with poison, and ideally the whale would end up dead on a nearby beach within a day or two. Whaling on the West Coast continued at this subsistence level for centuries, until widescale commercial whaling entered the region.

By the mid 1800s, European and American whalers were cruising the West Coast to hunt migrating whales. Shore-based Canadian industries on Vancouver Island and in the Gulf of Georgia were in operation from 1868 to 1872. After a short lull, the industry reopened in 1905, and there was always at least one company processing whales until the late 1960s. In 1967, the last shore-based whaling station in Canada was closed. It was the Coal Harbor station on the northern end of Vancouver Island, and although it had operated since 1911, only hints of that history can be seen there today.

ENVIRONMENTAL CONCERNS

To simply criticize whaling as ecologically unsound is to impose a modern awareness on an industry that historically was in great demand. The industry supported and initiated many advancements in society and technology, and even the expansion of the Industrial Revolution was facilitated by whale oil lubricants. Ironically, the whaling industry in British Columbia made extensive contributions to whale science, and it is this core of knowledge about whales that now helps us protect and understand them. We have made many efforts to save the great whales from further decline due to whaling, but other more subtle threats exist that may be as dangerous to whales as the harpoon.

A sad fact is that the oceans, which cover 70 percent of the planet, are being used as dumping grounds for a plethora of wastes and by-products produced by modern civilization. Far too many countries have intentionally and accidentally dumped harmful wastes into the oceans, believing that the water will somehow hide or deal with the garbage that no one else will accept. Unfortunately, the oceans are not capable of sanitizing or hiding the billions of tons of toxic waste, agricultural chemicals, crude oil and plastic debris that are carelessly dumped in, and these harmful substances are now affecting water quality and marine wildlife health around the world.

The magnitude of the problem is difficult to grasp. Many countries dump billions of tons of untreated waste water into the oceans. There are approximately 65,000 chemicals that are commonly used in industry worldwide, and all of these may end up in the oceans in some form or another. Chemical wastes—including DDT, organochlorides and heavy metals—stay in the environment for a long time. High concentrations can cause death of animals immediately, while low concentrations accumulate in the animal's tissues. Whales that eat small fish or plankton with toxic or chemical waste in their bodies end up storing these harmful substances in their blubber. In the worst cases, dolphins that have died from chemical poisoning and washed up on shore are so laden with pollutants that they themselves are classified as toxic waste. Also, a female's milk, which is made from the body's fat reserves, can be so full of organochlorides that the newborn calf dies. This kind of poisoning of the ocean and marine creatures is extremely insidious and difficult to remedy. It is essential to the health of the oceans that people are educated about how harmful wastes can be, and how to prevent the discharge from occurring.

One kind of pollution for which every person is responsible is plastic bags. Discarded plastic bags float in the water column and so closely resemble jellyfish and squid that many whales gulp them down. Eventually, a whale's digestive system is so blocked by plastic bags that it dies of starvation. Originally, when creatures that eat jellyfish or squid—such as whales and sea turtles—were found dead on shore, the cause of their deaths was unknown. It was only after autopsies that plastic bags were found to be the problem. Millions, or maybe even billions, of plastic bags are discarded every day, many of which will end up floating in the oceans.

There is no easy answer to the problem of marine pollution. Of course, the careless discarding of harmful products into the water must be curtailed, but the existing pollution in the water is not so easily cleaned up.

Fishing nets are also responsible for the deaths of innumerable cetaceans each year. The purse-seine nets commonly used for fishing often catch small whales, dolphins and porpoises. Once caught in a net underwater, a cetacean drowns because it must breathe air. When the nets are pulled in, the bodies of the drowned cetaceans must be untangled from the net. Eventually, a net is so full of holes that it is irreparable, and it is often discarded into the water. These discarded "ghost" nets continue to catch sea creatures and small cetaceans while they float freely through the ocean. Eventually a ghost net sinks to the bottom from the weight of the bodies trapped in its mesh. Large whales may become entangled in ghost nets too, and they end up towing the net with them wherever they go. The net ultimately digs into the whale's flesh, causing life-threatening injuries and preventing it from feeding properly.

Dolphin caught in fishing net

If you are out whale watching and you see a whale entangled in a fishing net, the best course of action is to report this whale and its location to an emergency hotline. The telephone numbers and addresses of people who will help an entangled whale are available at the back of this book (p. 156).

Extreme Whales

A simple truth about cetaceans is that many of their characteristics are difficult for us to understand. Their size, their weight, their communication—much of what makes a whale is unlike anything else we know. Typically, our efforts to understand whales involve compartmentalizing the information so that it is more manageable for us. We like to discuss large whales in terms of minimum and maximum lengths and weights, and we frequently discount reports of overly large whales as either myth or inaccurate reporting.

The framework in which we view whales, however, is not absolute. If the maximum length of a Blue Whale is reported by several authorities to be 100 ft (30 m), that does not preclude a whale of 105 ft (32 m), or more, from existing. In fact, there is much evidence to support the idea that large whales may keep getting slowly larger the older they get. Whalers of 100 and 200 years ago recorded enormous lengths for many whale species. Because whalers typically took the biggest whales (a simple choice to maximize profit for energy output) they would have also taken the oldest whales. Researchers commonly suggest that the reason we do not see such large specimens now is that the existing whales are comparatively young. Such a suggestion has to be based on the assumption that whales keep growing. Is this merely an assumption, or can it be proven scientifically?

LENGTH

Few animals demonstrate extended growth, but all that do share similar characteristics in their bone structure. For an animal to keep growing in length, the vertebral column must also be able to continue growing. Animals that stop growing soon after sexual maturity, such as humans, have vertebral columns that cannot grow anymore. On either side of each vertebra is a cap-like bone, called the epiphysis. While the animal is growing these "caps" are separated from the vertebra by a cartilaginous plate. For most mammals, after sexual maturity these "caps" fuse to the vertebra and growing (in length) stops. For large whales, such as the rorquals, this fusion is greatly delayed after sexual maturity and many older whales that are caught still have unfused epiphyses.

Given this evidence, it should not be surprising to find accounts of extremely large whales. For small whales, dolphins and porpoises, the epiphyses probably do fuse early and they have maximum lengths. In most cases, the measurements in this book indicate the maximum records for each species, as well as the average. This average is the most likely size of whale for each species that you will see while out whale watching. A truth about nature is that there are always exceptions. For example, the maximum length stated herein for the Humpback Whale is 62 ft (19 m). This figure represents a reasonable maximum for the species. However, a female Humpback was once captured in shallow waters near Bermuda that measured a staggering 88 ft (27 m). Exceptional whales do exist, and they remind us that our measurements and descriptions are only guides, not rules.

DIVING DEPTH

Other whale extremes are also well documented. For example, the depth to which Sperm Whales can dive, or the weights of the large rorqual, Bowhead and right whales are all subject to revision as we discover greater or more exceptional examples. Good science is about taking new information and shifting our framework to encompass it, rather than discounting evidence as mere calculation error or myth. The weight of large whales is very difficult to determine, but we can reasonably assume that the larger a whale specimen is, the more it is going to weigh.

The maximum weights recorded in this book are from unusually large whales. The generally accepted average weight is also included, and this figure corresponds to the average length. Sperm Whales were once thought to dive to a maximum depth of about 5000 ft (1500 m). We now accept that Sperm Whales can dive much deeper. One of the deepest records is from two Sperm Whale males that were killed upon surfacing from water that was 10,500 ft (3200 m) deep. They both had freshly eaten bottom-dwelling sharks in their stomachs, indicating that Sperm Whales can dive as deep as this. Perhaps there is no maximum: the Sperm Whale is perfectly adapted to handle the stress of deep diving, and the determining factor of the dive depth may be availability of food or time without oxygen.

LONGEVITY

Current research on Bowhead Whales has turned up startling evidence that these arctic-dwelling whales may live for more than 200 years. Interest in Bowheads sparked when Inupiat hunters found old spearpoints and arrowheads buried deep in the flesh of a few individuals. Some of these stone points are dated at up to 200 years old, indicating the whale could be several years older than that. The traditional methods used by researchers to determine the age of a whale do not work on Bowhead Whales. A new method that studies the delicate layering in the lens of the eye is being employed to determine Bowhead ages. This method has shown several individuals at 150 years or more, and at least one at 215 years old. We do not know the maximum life span of a Bowhead Whale, and some researchers suggest that 215 may still be conservative. At more than 200 years old, Bowhead Whales are now considered some of the longest-lived creatures on Earth, together with Giant Tortoises (150 years old, with disputed records at up to 200 years old) and Giant Clams (up to 220 years old).

WHALES vs. DINOSAURS

It is a popular belief that whales are bigger than dinosaurs. Although whales can be accurately measured for length, weighing these beasts is nearly impossible. As for dinosaurs, measuring their length involves speculation and educated guessing. Many dinosaur species are known only from a few separate bones, and determining the length of a complete animal is sheer inference. To complicate matters, paleontologists keep turning up larger and larger specimens. No one even knows which species is the biggest dinosaur. Weighing a dinosaur is, of course, impossible and any given measurement is only theory.

Certain rules in biology make this guessing game easier. We know, for example, that a marine animal can generally have a greater body mass than a land animal, because the water helps support the weight. The conclusion is that Blue Whales—at up to 200 tons (181,400 kg)—win as the heaviest creatures, while certain dinosaurs are the longest creatures that ever lived. The longest dinosaurs known include the Supersaurus, at 100–130 ft (30–40 m), and both the Seismosaurus and recently discovered Argentinosaurus, at 110–160 ft (34–49 m).

hale Tales & Record Breakers

This section attempts to clarify some of the frequently asked questions about whales and whale extremes. Keep in mind, however, that these answers are not absolute. As we learn and discover more about the marine world, we have to continually update our record sheets.

HOW MANY DIFFERENT WHALES ARE IN THE WORLD?
There are currently 81 known species of whales, dolphins and porpoises.

WHAT IS THE LARGEST WHALE IN THE WORLD?
Blue Whale: maximum record 110 ft (34 m).

WHAT IS THE SMALLEST WHALE IN THE WORLD?
Franciscana (river dolphin): 4^1/$_2$–6 ft (1.4–1.8 m).

WHAT IS THE HEAVIEST WHALE IN THE WORLD?
Blue Whale: maximum record 200 tons (181,400 kg).

WHAT IS THE LONGEST-LIVED WHALE?
Bowhead Whale: more than 200 years.

WHAT IS A WHALE SHARK?
A Whale Shark is a shark, not a whale. The modifier "whale" is used because this shark is very big (up to 60 ft [18 m] long).

WHAT IS THE FASTEST WHALE IN THE WORLD?
Atlantic White-sided Dolphin: 32 knots (59 km/h).

WHAT IS THE DEEPEST-DIVING WHALE?
Sperm Whale: deepest record 10,000 ft (3050 m).

HOW LONG CAN WHALES HOLD THEIR BREATH?
Sperm Whale: confirmed record 2 hours 18 minutes.

HOW MUCH FOOD CAN A WHALE EAT IN ONE DAY?
Blue Whale: up to 8 tons (7300 kg).

WHAT IS THE LONGEST MIGRATION MADE BY A WHALE?
Gray Whale: round trip (one year) 12,400 mi (20,000 km).

WHAT IS THE LONGEST PREGNANCY FOR A WHALE?
Orca: 15 to 16 months.

WHAT IS THE RAREST WHALE IN THE WORLD?
Yangtze River Dolphin (China): fewer than 100 remaining.

WHAT IS THE LOUDEST SOUND MADE BY A WHALE?
Blue Whale: 188 decibels, measurable for at least 1500 mi (2400 km) underwater.

WHICH WHALE HAS THE MOST BALEEN PLATES (ON AVERAGE)?
Fin Whale: 360 plates.

WHICH WHALE HAS THE MOST TEETH?
Spinner Dolphin: 224.

WHICH WHALE HAS THE LONGEST TEETH?
Narwhal: a single tusk can reach 10 ft (3 m) long. One in 500 males have two tusks.

WHICH WHALE HAS THE LONGEST BALEEN?
Bowhead Whale: 14 ft (4.3 m). One disputed report of baleen measuring 19 ft (5.8 m) in length.

Baleen Whales

GRAY WHALE FAMILY (ESCHRICHTIIDAE)

The Gray Whale, which is the sole member of this family, shares some characteristics with both right whales and rorquals: like a right whale, the Gray Whale has a heavy appearance and an arched mouth; like a rorqual, it has throat pleats (although fewer and less effective ones) that expand when food-rich water is drawn into the mouth. Overall, the Gray Whale is a mottled gray color, bespeckled with many patches of callosities and barnacles. The Gray Whale is believed to carry more parasites, such as barnacles and whale lice, than any other whale.

Gray Whale

RORQUAL FAMILY (BALAENOPTERIDAE)

The rorquals, numbering only a few species worldwide, include some of the largest whales on earth—the Blue Whale is reputed to be one of the largest animals that has ever lived. The name "rorqual" is derived from the Norwegian word *rorhval*, meaning "furrow," and refers to the pleats, or folds, in the skin of the throat. These throat pleats expand during feeding, allowing the throat to distend to an enormous, balloon-like shape when the whale gulps a massive volume of food-rich water into its mouth. The whale does not swallow the water; instead, the pleats contract and the tongue moves forward to push the water out through the baleen. Any crustaceans or fish are trapped inside the mouth to be swallowed whole. The only whales outside the rorqual family that have throat pleats are the Gray Whale and beaked whales, but their pleats are relatively few and have greatly reduced efficacy.

Fin Whale

There are six members in this family, five of which may be seen off the coast of British Columbia or Alaska. Rorquals are easily identified by their pointed snouts, flattened heads, long, slender bodies and relatively small dorsal fins, which are set about two-thirds of the way down the back. When a rorqual's mouth is open, the short baleen, which is continuous around the forward point of the jaw, is visible.

RIGHT WHALE FAMILY (BALAENIDAE)

This family includes two kinds of whales, the Bowhead Whale and the right whales. The Bowhead Whale is found only in arctic and subarctic waters. Right whales have a much larger distribution.

The endangered right whales were once found throughout the world's cold and temperate oceans. Their total population now is probably only a few thousand individuals. There is much argument about whether there are one, two or even three species of right whales. Many scientists believe there is only one species worldwide, *Balaena glacialis*, while others feel strongly that this represents only the northern population, and that the Southern Hemisphere has a different species, *B. australis*.

Among the most distinct features of a right whale are the growths over its face and head. These callosities are masses of keratin topped with barnacles and teeming with whale lice. The whale lice may be pink, white, orange or yellow, and therefore give the callosities their unique color. The origin of these callosities is intriguing—they grow in all the places on the whale's head where a human would have hair. Specifically, they are found on the chin, the upper "lip," the top of the rostrum and above the eye. Keratin makes up both fingernails and hair in other mammals, and this may explain the origin of callosities in right whales.

Bowhead Whales do not have callosities like the right whales do, so their appearance is sleek and smooth. Their jaw line is more rounded than that of right whales, and their baleen is slightly longer. Bowhead baleen was eagerly sought for many decades. Commercial hunting of Bowheads greatly reduced their population, but in recent years their numbers have improved.

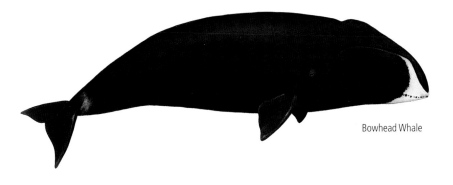

Bowhead Whale

Gray Whale

Eschrichtius robustus

Gray Whales, which are among the most frequently observed whales, are famous for their extensive migrations. Almost the entire world population of Gray Whales travels back and forth between the cold arctic seas where they spend summer and the warm Mexican waters where they spend winter, which amounts to about 12,400 mi (20,000 km) a year. A separate, small population of Gray Whales spends its summers in the Sea of Okhotsk off Siberia and migrates to the southern tip of Korea for winter.

During their summers in arctic or near-arctic seas, Gray Whales feed on amphipods, which are abundant bottom-dwelling crustaceans. These whales eat enormous quantities of food during their five to six months in the north to put on as much weight as possible. In migration, and especially during their stay in southern waters, they eat very little, and they may even fast completely. A Gray Whale can lose as much as 30 percent of its body weight between summers, and it is slim and hungry when it returns to the food-rich waters of the Arctic in early summer.

The Gray Whales' southward journey takes approximately three months: they leave the Arctic by late September and arrive in the waters off southern California and Mexico by late December. This migration coincides with the reproductive activity of the whales, and once in the warm waters, most females either mate or give birth. By late February or March, Gray Whales begin their return to northern waters.

DIVE SEQUENCE

BALEEN WHALES

RANGE: Gray Whales are now found only in the coastal waters of the North Pacific, primarily along the western coast of North America. A small population occurs along the eastern coast of Asia.

OTHER NAMES: Devilfish, Mussel-digger, Scrag Whale

STATUS: Endangered (USFWS); locally common in British Columbia and Alaska

TOTAL LENGTH: up to 50 ft (15 m); average 45 ft (14 m)

TOTAL WEIGHT: up to 45 tons (41,000 kg); average 35 tons (32,000 kg)

BIRTH LENGTH: about 15 ft (4.6 m)

BIRTH WEIGHT: 1000 lb (450 kg)

Mothers with new calves may postpone their departure just a bit longer to ensure that their young have the strength for the journey. The Gray Whales arrive in the Arctic again by May or June.

The Gray Whale, which once inhabited both the Atlantic and Pacific oceans, has been close to extinction at least twice in human history, and it now lives only in Pacific waters. The main reason for its decline was the whaling industry—the Gray Whale lives primarily in shallow waters, so it was an easy target. Aside from humans, the only predator of the Gray Whale is the Orca (p. 86), which might take young or weak individuals. Now that Gray Whale populations are carefully protected, they are slowly recovering their numbers. The Gray Whale can be quite tolerant of humans, and it may even approach boats, which makes it a favorite of whale watchers throughout the West Coast.

DESCRIPTION: The Gray Whale is easily distinguished from other whales by its mottled gray appearance and its narrow, triangular head. The head is slightly arched between the eye and the tip of the snout, and the jaw line usually has a similar arch. Like a rorqual, the Gray Whale has throat pleats—typically only two pleats, however, although three to seven are not uncommon. Over most of the body, but especially on the head, there are many yellow, orange or whitish patches of crusted barnacles or lice. The flippers, which are relatively small, are wide at the base but taper to a pointed tip. There is no dorsal fin, but there is a large bump where the dorsal fin should be and then a series of smaller bumps, or "knuckles," continuing along the dorsal ridge to the tail. The tail is distinctly notched and has pointed flukes. Female Gray Whales are generally larger than males.

BLOW: When viewed from the front or the rear, the Gray Whale's blow, which can be up to 15 ft (4.6 m) high, is bushy and heart-shaped. In some cases, the blow looks V-shaped. From the side view, the blow is bushy but not distinctive.

OTHER DISPLAYS: The Gray Whale actively partakes in breaching, spy-hopping and fluking. It will breach anywhere in its range, but most often in breeding lagoons in the south, often two or three times in a row. It rises nearly vertically out of the water and then comes down with an enormous splash. Spy-hopping is also common, and this whale may keep its head out of the water for 30 seconds or more. In shallow water, a Gray Whale may "cheat" and rest its flukes on the bottom so it can keep its head above water powerful tongue to push the silty water out through the baleen, trapping all the crustaceans inside. Most Gray Whales are "right-lipped"—as most humans are right-handed—and prefer to feed using the right side of the mouth. A close-up look at a Gray Whale's face will reveal its "handedness," because its preferred side will have numerous white scars and no barnacles. Inside the whale's mouth, the same uneven wear is visible in the baleen: on "right-lipped" whales, the baleen plates on the right side are more worn and shorter than the plates on the left.

REPRODUCTION: Gray Whales mate in December or January, and a single young is born 13$^{1}/_{2}$ months later—in the following January or February. The young travel northward with their mother when they are only two months old, and they continue nursing until they are six to nine months old. Male Gray Whales are sexually mature when they are just over 36 ft (11 m) long; females are sexually mature when they are nearly 38 ft (12 m) long.

with minimal effort. Before a deep dive, this whale raises its flukes clear above the surface of the water. As it descends, the bumps along its dorsal ridge are visible, as are its distinctly notched tail and pointed flukes.

GROUP SIZE: Generally, this whale is seen in groups of only one to three individuals. It may migrate in groups of up to 15 individuals, and food-rich areas in the north can attract dozens or hundreds of Gray Whales at one time.

FEEDING: Unlike other baleen whales, the Gray Whale is primarily a bottom feeder. Its food consists of benthic amphipods and other bottom-dwelling invertebrates. A feeding whale dives down to the bottom and rolls onto one side, sticking out its lower lip and sucking in great volumes of food, water and muck. Once its mouth is full, it uses its

Humpback Whale

SIMILAR SPECIES:
Humpback Whale (p. 54).

Minke Whale

Balaenoptera acutorostrata

The Minke Whale, the smallest of the rorquals, is a relatively common whale of the West Coast and arctic seas. Despite its numbers, the Minke Whale is elusive and difficult to spot, because it spends less time at the surface than other whales—it usually takes only five to seven breaths before it goes under again. As well, the Minke Whale usually travels singly, and one little dorsal fin against an ocean of waves is easy to overlook. On the other hand, there are cases where a Minke Whale has surfaced right next to a boat, much to the surprise of the people aboard. Such occurrences are fleeting: the whale takes a quick breath and disappears as quickly as it came.

Several researchers who have studied Minke Whales consider them extremely intelligent and adaptable. In some cases, Minke Whales look for flocks of gulls, murres or auklets on the water—a flock of feeding birds advertises the whereabouts of a school of fish, making the fish an easy lunch for the whale. Although Minke Whales in central and southern oceans frequently use this tricky technique, the behavior is not common in northern waters.

The study of Minke Whales is still in its early stages, owing partly to the elusiveness of the animal, but also to its wide distribution. People wanting to study Gray Whales, for example, know exactly where to find Gray Whales, but Minke Whales can be anywhere and we have yet to determine their behavior patterns.

DIVE SEQUENCE

RANGE: The Minke Whale is found in every ocean of the world. In summer it is common in cold polar waters; in winter it migrates to more temperate waters.

OTHER NAMES: Piked Whale, Sharp-headed Finner, Little Finner, Lesser Finback, Lesser Rorqual

STATUS: Locally common; insufficient data worldwide

TOTAL LENGTH: up to 35 ft (11 m); average 27 ft (8.2 m)

TOTAL WEIGHT: up to 15 tons (14,000 kg); average 10 tons (9000 kg)

BIRTH LENGTH: 8–9 ft (2.4–2.7 m)

BIRTH WEIGHT: 770 lb (350 kg)

It is known that many Minke Whales migrate between warm and cold waters each year, but some whales are believed to stay in one region year-round. The Minke Whale's winter mating and calving waters in the North Pacific remain a mystery. New advances in satellite technology and radio markers, however, may help answer some of these questions.

In the 1980s, the Minke Whale was the most heavily hunted baleen whale in the world. The populations of the larger whales had declined so dramatically by that time that whalers from many countries started to take this small rorqual instead. The Minke is still more heavily hunted than almost any other whale, but new regulations and international efforts have protected it in many parts of its range.

DESCRIPTION: The Minke Whale is a striking whale with whorls of white over its dark back and with white "epaulettes" on its flippers. On some individuals, the entire flipper may be white; on others, the white may be just a narrow band or even nonexistent. This variation in flipper markings is regionally specific, and it might indicate different subspecies. The coloration over the back varies considerably throughout the Minke's range: it can be dark slate gray, nearly black, deep bluish or dark brown. A Minke Whale's undersides are white or nearly white, and there are often swirls of white behind the flippers and again below the dorsal fin. This whale's overall appearance in the water is very sleek and streamlined. Its head is quite pointed, with a prominent splashguard before the blowhole and a distinct, single ridge to the snout. Relative to most other rorquals, a Minke Whale has a large, curved dorsal fin. Female Minke Whales are generally larger than males.

BLOW: The Minke Whale makes a small, quick, bushy blow that reaches a maximum height of about 9 ft

Flipper variations

BALEEN WHALES

FEEDING: Like the larger rorquals, the Minke Whale feeds mainly on krill, but it also eats some other invertebrates and small fish. It commonly lunge-feeds by swimming into a school of krill or small fish and gulping a large volume of food-filled water into its mouth. Its throat stretches like a big balloon, and as the whale closes its mouth and contracts the throat pleats, the water is forced out through the baleen. The organisms in the water are trapped in the mouth, and the whale uses its tongue to wipe the creatures off the baleen so it can swallow them.

REPRODUCTION: Minkes probably mate in late winter, but no calving waters have been found and very little is known about their reproductive cycle. The gestation period is 10 months. The nursing period is probably very short, because the calves are weaned before they arrive at the summer waters. Male Minke Whales are sexually mature when they reach about 23 ft (7 m) in length; females when they are 24 ft (7.3 m) long.

(2.7 m). The blow may not be visible, because it disperses quickly. On a very calm day, you may hear the blow rather than see it.

OTHER DISPLAYS: When a Minke Whale breaches, it comes far enough out of the water to expose its dorsal fin. The whale leaves the water at about a 45° angle, and it usually does not twist or turn as it comes down with a tremendous splash. This whale often arches back into the water headfirst, so the breach looks more like a dive than a belly flop.

GROUP SIZE: Minke Whales are seen either singly or in groups of two to four individuals. In areas of high food concentrations, a hundred or more Minke Whales may occur together.

Sei Whale

SIMILAR SPECIES: Sei Whale (p. 46); Fin Whale (p. 48).

Sei Whale

Balaenoptera borealis

DESCRIPTION: The Sei Whale is very similar to the larger Fin Whale (p. 48), and the two are hard to distinguish in the open ocean. The Sei Whale is mainly dark gray, blackish or bluish gray, with pale gray or whitish undersides, and it may have irregular, pale scars and marks along its body. Its baleen is finer and silkier than that of other rorquals, and its throat pleats are shorter. The dorsal fin is slender, upright and curved on the trailing edge. The flippers are dark on both sides, and they have pointed tips. The tail flukes are small relative to the size of the body. Female Sei Whales are generally larger than males.

OTHER DISPLAYS: Sei Whales breach infrequently, and rarely more than once at a time. They leave the water at a low angle and re-enter with a splash.

GROUP SIZE: Sei Whales are seen either singly or in groups of up to five individuals. Feeding waters attract larger numbers.

FEEDING: The Sei Whale feeds primarily on shoals or swarms of small fish or invertebrates, such as squid, krill and copepods. Its feeding style is similar to a right whale's: rather than lunge-feeding like the other rorquals, the Sei Whale skims steadily through food-rich water.

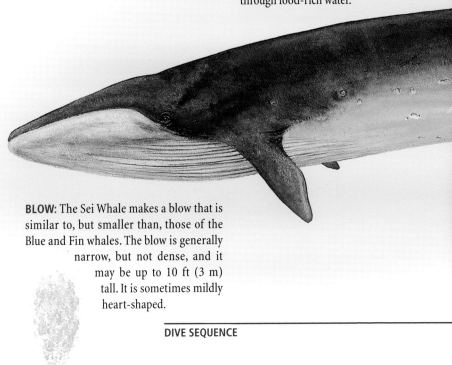

BLOW: The Sei Whale makes a blow that is similar to, but smaller than, those of the Blue and Fin whales. The blow is generally narrow, but not dense, and it may be up to 10 ft (3 m) tall. It is sometimes mildly heart-shaped.

DIVE SEQUENCE

RANGE: Sei Whales are found in deep, temperate waters worldwide. In summer, they may feed in subpolar waters, but they usually occur in lower latitudes.

OTHER NAMES: Pollack Whale, Coalfish Whale, Sardine Whale, Japan Finner, Boreal Rorqual, Rudolphi's Rorqual

STATUS: Endangered (USFWS)

TOTAL LENGTH: up to 69 ft (21 m); average 48 ft (15 m)

TOTAL WEIGHT: average 35 tons (32,000 kg)

BIRTH LENGTH: 14–16 ft (4.3–4.9 m)

BIRTH WEIGHT: about 1600 lb (730 kg)

Minke Whale

REPRODUCTION: Sei Whales mate and bear their young in mid-winter. The gestation period is 11½ months. The calves are born singly. These whales are sexually mature when they are about 95 percent of their total adult length.

SIMILAR SPECIES: Minke Whale (p. 42); Fin Whale (p. 48); Blue Whale (p. 50).

Fin Whale

Balaenoptera physalus

DESCRIPTION: The unusual Fin Whale has a striking asymmetry of coloration on its head: the right side of the outer lower "lip" and the baleen on the right side are whitish, while the counterparts on the left side are gray. Oddly enough, the mouth cavity and tongue are gray on the right and white on the left. There is a distinct, pale gray, V-shaped mark behind the head. The overall body color is dark gray, silvery gray or brownish black, with white undersides. The dorsal fin is small and slanted backward. The flippers and flukes are dark on top and white below. There is a distinct ridge on the back from the dorsal fin to the flukes. Female Fin Whales are generally larger than males.

OTHER DISPLAYS: Fin Whales may make spectacular breaches, leaving the water at 45°, but they rarely show their dorsal fins. They may twist in the air as they come down with a thunderous splash.

GROUP SIZE: Fin Whales are occasionally found singly or in pairs, but typically in groups of 3 to 10 individuals.

BLOW: The Fin Whale's narrow blow is quite dense and is 13–20 ft (4–6.1 m) high, making it visible from far away.

DIVE SEQUENCE

BALEEN WHALES

RANGE: Fin Whales are found worldwide in temperate and subpolar waters. They are more common in the Southern Hemisphere.

OTHER NAMES: Common Rorqual, Finback, Razorback, Herring Whale, Finner

STATUS: Endangered (USFWS)

TOTAL LENGTH: up to 89 ft (27 m); average 70 ft (21 m)

TOTAL WEIGHT: up to 140 tons (127,000 kg); average 80 tons (73,000 kg)

BIRTH LENGTH: 20–22 ft (6.1–6.7 m)

BIRTH WEIGHT: about 2 tons (1800 kg)

FEEDING: The main diet of the Fin Whale includes schooling fish, krill, squid, copepods and other invertebrates. Lunge-feeding is commonly seen, during which the whale often turns on its right side.

REPRODUCTION: Fin Whales mate in late winter. About 11 months later a single calf is born. Males are sexually mature at 90 percent of their adult length; females at 75 to 80 percent.

Blue Whale

SIMILAR SPECIES: Blue Whale (p. 50); Sei Whale (p. 46).

Blue Whale

Balaenoptera musculus

Bigger than a dinosaur, bigger than a jet plane, bigger than three school buses—the words we use to describe the size of the Blue Whale hardly do justice to this leviathan. We cannot easily comprehend or describe how large the Blue Whale is, and perhaps this difficulty is reflected in the 18th-century humor used to name the species scientifically. As if in jest because any word we could use to describe this whale would fall short of capturing its true immensity, the Latin word *musculus*, meaning "little mouse," was used. The Blue Whale is so manifestly not a mouse that we can only smile at the comparison.

The Blue Whale is the most famous record-breaker in the animal kingdom. Not only is it the largest creature alive, and maybe the largest there ever has been, but it is also the loudest—its low-frequency pulses have been measured at up to 188 decibels. At birth, a Blue Whale calf is 23 ft (7 m) long, which is already larger than at least two-thirds of whales at their full adult length, even though the gestation period—about a year—is pretty typical of whales. The calf grows at an incredible rate: it puts on a staggering 200 lb (91 kg) a day, nursing 50 gal (190 *l*) of milk from its mother every 24 hours, and a weaned juvenile (about 1^1/$_2$ years old) is about 50 ft (15 m) long. As adults, the largest individuals may eat up to 8 tons (7300 kg) of food a day during summer. Their hearts are as large as a car, and a small child could crawl through their arteries. A male's penis is about 10 ft (3 m) long.

Another record the Blue Whale holds, unfortunately, is that it is one of the most endangered large cetaceans on Earth. The height of the whaling industry in the late 1800s and early 1900s generated a relentless pursuit of Blue Whales.

DIVE SEQUENCE

RANGE: Blue Whales are usually found in open waters. Although their distribution appears to be worldwide, it is not continuous.

OTHER NAMES: Sulfur-bottom, Sibbald's Rorqual, Great Northern Rorqual

STATUS: Endangered (USFWS)

TOTAL LENGTH: up to 110 ft (34 m); average 85 ft (26 m)

TOTAL WEIGHT: up to 200 tons (181,000 kg); average 120 tons (109,000 kg)

BIRTH LENGTH: about 23 ft (7 m)

BIRTH WEIGHT: about 2.5 tons (2300 kg)

By 1950, the species was declared endangered. In 1966, the International Whaling Commission gave a protected status to the Blue Whale, and it is slowly recovering. The total population is at least 6000, but there may be as many as 11,000 individuals.

The natural history of the Blue Whale is not well documented. Studies in the wild are difficult to undertake, and the bodies of stranded or hunted animals reveal limited information. In general, the Blue Whale migrates from low-latitude winter waters to high-latitude summer waters. Some populations, such as the one in the northern Indian Ocean, may reside year-round in the same place.

There are thought to be three subspecies of the Blue Whale: our West Coast Blues belong to the subspecies *B. m. musculus*; the largest Blue Whales, *B. m. intermedia*, grow up to 110 ft (34 m) and are found in the Southern Hemisphere; the smallest, *B. m. brevicauda*, which grow to (only) 73 ft (22 m) and are often called Pygmy Blue Whales, occur in the tropical waters of the Southern Hemisphere.

DESCRIPTION: The enormous Blue Whale is typically deep slate blue or grayish in color, with variable pale gray or white mottling over the back. Its undersides are lighter, and range in color from pale blue gray to white to yellowish. A film of diatoms on the pale undersides results in yellowish bellies on some individuals and gives rise to the alternate name "sulfur-bottom." The Blue Whale has a broad, flattened head, a large splash-guard before the blowhole, and a pale throat with 55 to 88 pleats. The relatively tiny dorsal fin is located about three-quarters of the way down the body. The flippers are long, slender and darker above than below. The tail stock is very thick. The flukes are narrow, slightly notched and very wide—almost one-quarter of the body length. Female Blue Whales are generally larger than males.

side or belly. An adult's dive sequence is marked initially by the tall blow; then the whale's long back rolls over the surface. The dorsal fin appears well after the head has disappeared and the blow has dispersed. During its dive sequence, a Blue Whale may surface several times over a period of up to six minutes, and then it will dive for 10 to 20 minutes or longer.

GROUP SIZE: Blue Whales are typically seen in groups of one to five individuals, although good feeding waters can attract several more.

FEEDING: The Blue Whale specializes in eating krill—shrimp-like creatures that are about 2 in (5.1 cm) in length—and it rarely eats anything else. A Blue Whale usually rises up into a school of krill from below, gulping in hundreds of gallons of seawater. The water is squeezed out through the baleen either rapidly or over the course of several minutes.

REPRODUCTION: Gestation lasts 11 to 12 months for Blue Whales, and the peak calving period appears to be during winter, when the whales are at low latitudes. Calves are weaned when they are about eight months old. Both sexes reach sexual maturity when they are at least 80 percent of their adult length—about 10 years old.

BLOW: The blow of the Blue Whale is unmistakable: the narrow column of spray can rise at least 35 ft (11 m) high, and it can be seen even at a distance.

OTHER DISPLAYS: Not surprisingly, the Blue Whale is not acrobatic, although a juvenile may breach and make a tremendous splash as it falls back into the water, either on its

Fin Whale

SIMILAR SPECIES:
Fin Whale (p. 48); Sei Whale (p. 46).

53

Humpback Whale

Megaptera novaeangliae

Humpback Whales are renowned for both their extensive migrations and their haunting songs. They are commonly seen by whale watchers, and they seem to enjoy performing for their boat-bound admirers. Other than brief bouts of fighting between males during the winter breeding season, Humpback Whales have gentle and docile natures.

One of the most famous places for viewing Humpbacks is the Pacific Northwest, where many of them spend their summers. When winter sets in, Humpback Whales migrate to the warm waters of either Hawaii or Mexico, and they may alternate their destination each year. As much as 5000 mi (8000 km) can lie between their high-latitude feeding waters and their tropical mating and calving waters. Humpbacks only feed in the summer, and after their winter in the tropics they are slim and hungry.

The song of the Humpback Whale is one of the most impressive sounds in the animal kingdom. A Humpback can sing for a few minutes to half an hour, and an entire performance can go on for several days, with only short breaks between each song. The

DIVE SEQUENCE

RANGE: Humpback Whales are found throughout the world from polar to tropical waters. They migrate seasonally, so some regions have higher densities than others.

STATUS: Endangered (USFWS); threatened (COSEWIC); locally common off British Columbia and Alaska

TOTAL LENGTH: up to 62 ft (19 m); average 45 ft (14 m)

TOTAL WEIGHT: up to 53 tons (48,000 kg); average 30 tons (27,000 kg)

BIRTH LENGTH: 13–16 ft (4–4.9 m)

BIRTH WEIGHT: 1–2 tons (900–1800 kg)

songs are composed of trills, whines, snores, wheezes and sighs, and when sung in a repeating pattern, the result is mysterious and hauntingly beautiful. While the true meaning of the Humpback's song eludes us, we do know that only the males sing and that they perform mainly during the breeding season. Many animals use sound to attract the opposite sex, which may be the primary function of the songs.

Male Humpbacks become very aggressive toward one another and battle to determine dominance on their winter breeding grounds. A dominant male becomes the escort to a female with a calf. Presumably, a female with a calf is one that is, or will soon be, receptive to mating.

DESCRIPTION: The Humpback Whale is slightly more robust in the body than other rorquals. The overall body color is either dark gray or dark slate blue, and the undersides may be the same color as the back or nearly white. The slender head bears many knobs and projections around the snout, and the mouth line arches downward to the eye. There are 12 to 36 pleats on the pale throat. The flippers are long and knobby and have a varying pattern of white markings. The tail flukes are strongly swept back and have irregular trailing edges. Like the flippers, the flukes have unique white markings that can be used to identify individual whales. The dorsal fin can be small or stubby or high and curved, and several small knuckles are visible on the dorsal ridge between the fin and the tail. Humpbacks often host barnacles and whale lice. Female Humpbacks are generally larger than males.

Fluke variations

BALEEN WHALES

often inquisitive, and they may approach boats if boaters are non-harassing. When they breathe and dive, they roll through the water and show a strongly arched back. The tail flukes are lifted high only on deep dives.

GROUP SIZE: Humpbacks commonly live in small groups of two or three members, but some groups may have 15 members, and Humpbacks are occasionally seen singly. Good feeding and breeding waters usually draw large groups.

FEEDING: The Humpback Whale mainly feeds by lunge-feeding or bubble-netting, but much individual variation occurs in feeding styles. Its major foods are krill and schooling fish, such as herring, sand lance and capelin.

REPRODUCTION: The courtship behavior of Humpbacks is elaborate and involves lengthy bouts of singing by the males. Mating usually occurs in warm waters, and single calves are born following a gestation of about $11^1/_2$ months. The calves stay close to their mothers and nurse for about one year. Females reach sexual maturity when they are about 40 ft (12 m) long and males when they are at least 38 ft (12 m) long.

BLOW: The Humpback Whale makes a thick, orb-shaped blow that can reach up to 10 ft (3 m) high and is visible at a great distance. From directly in front or behind, the blow may appear slightly heart-shaped.

OTHER DISPLAYS: An acrobatic whale, the Humpback dazzles whale watchers with high breaches that finish in a tremendous splash. Other behaviors that it may repeat several times include lob-tailing, flipper-slapping and spy-hopping. Humpbacks are

Gray Whale

SIMILAR SPECIES: Gray Whale (p. 38).

Northern Right Whale

Balaena glacialis

This highly endangered animal was the most heavily pursued whale during the height of whaling. The name "right whale" is derived from mariners referring to it as the "right" whale to hunt: it is large, it has thick blubber and long baleen; and it swims slowly. The Northern Right Whale was the first whale to be hunted commercially, and hundreds of thousands of right whales were killed to feed the demand for whale oil and other whale products. By 1920, the Northern Right Whale was nearly extinct. There are still only about 200 right whales in the North Pacific and perhaps just 300 in the North Atlantic. In the Southern Hemisphere, the numbers are better—as many as 3000 Southern Right Whales (*B. australis*) still exist. The chances of seeing a Northern Right Whale along the West Coast are slim, but if such a sighting occurs and is confirmed, please make sure it is reported to the nearest marine research station.

When Northern Right Whales are seen in the wild, they can be quite approachable and inquisitive. Sometimes these whales are playful and bump and push floating objects in the water. As a cautionary note, these qualities of inquisitiveness and playfulness can result in a whale playing near or with your boat. Some kayakers have been surprised when their little boat was bumped or lifted in friendly jest.

DIVE SEQUENCE

RANGE: Northern Right Whales are found in polar and temperate waters of the Northern Hemisphere. They favor offshore waters rather than the open ocean.

OTHER NAMES: Black Right Whale, Biscayan Right Whale

STATUS: Critically endangered (USFWS/COSEWIC)

TOTAL LENGTH: up to 60 ft (18 m); average 45 ft (14 m)

TOTAL WEIGHT: up to 95 tons (86,000 kg); average 60 tons (54,000 kg)

BIRTH LENGTH: 15–20 ft (4.6–6.1 m)

BIRTH WEIGHT: about 1 ton (910 kg)

BALEEN WHALES

As everyone knows, the greatest record-breaking animal in the world is the Blue Whale. The understated Northern Right Whale, however, wins a few titles of its own. While not a very noble title of recognition, the Northern Right Whale may well be the slowest whale on Earth. Less charitable still, it is one of the most robust (or fattest) whales, considering its weight per foot of body length. Its large tail is the broadest of all, relative to the length of the body. The one title this whale carries that may place it in the realm of nobility among cetaceans is for the largest testicles. With testes weighing in at 1 ton (910 kg), no other creature in the history of the world is as well-endowed. By comparison, the testes of the now-humbled Blue Whale weigh a mere 150 lb (68 kg).

DESCRIPTION: The robust Northern Right Whale is easy to distinguish because of the callosities on its head and its lack of a dorsal fin. Distinct callosities grow on the chin, on the rostrum, in front of the blowhole and above the eye. The body is nearly black, dark blue or dark brown, and it may show slight mottling or even patchy white spots on the belly. The mouth line is strongly arched upward and then drops nearly vertically to meet the eye. There is a distinct indent behind the blowhole and then a bulge continuing over the back. The baleen plates can be as long as 8 ft (2.4 m). The flippers are large and spatula-shaped, and they are dark on both sides. At close range, the finger bones in a flipper can be seen as distinct ridges. The flukes, also dark both above and below, are smooth, pointed and have a noticeable notch in the middle. Female Northern Right Whales are generally larger than males.

BLOW: When viewed from the front or the rear, the right whale's distinctive blow is widely V-shaped. The sound is loud, and the spray can reach a height of 16 ft (4.9 m).

OTHER DISPLAYS: The Northern Right Whale is quite acrobatic considering its bulk. It often breaches, lob-tails, flipper-slaps and spy-hops. When it lob-tails, it may invert in the water to such a great extent that it appears to be doing a headstand.

hairs of the baleen plates and eventually swallowed. This whale skim-feeds wherever the food is present—at the surface or at depth.

REPRODUCTION: The Northern Right Whale has never managed to recover its numbers the way other whales have. The reasons are not clear, but the combination of isolated populations and a slow reproductive rate may be responsible. Females give birth only once every three or four years. Although these whales court and mate year-round, peak conception appears to be in winter, as is calving, which indicates a gestation period of about one year. Both sexes are sexually mature when they are 75 to 80 percent of the adult length.

GROUP SIZE: These right whales are typically found in small groups of two or three individuals. Sometimes a group numbering up to 12 members is seen. Seasonal feeding waters attract larger numbers of whales at certain times.

FEEDING: A remarkably efficient filter-feeder, the Northern Right Whale feeds on some of the smallest zooplankton in the sea. The primary food is tiny krill and other copepods. To feed, the whale swims slowly with its mouth open. The unique shape of the baleen makes the mouth look like a cave. As the whale progresses through a concentration of copepods, the water enters the "cave" and passes through the baleen. All of the creatures are trapped against the silky

Bowhead Whale

SIMILAR SPECIES: Bowhead Whale (p. 62).

Bowhead Whale

Balaena mysticetus

DESCRIPTION: The Bowhead Whale is a large, rotund whale with a strongly bowed mouth line. It is mainly black in color, although it may have a white chin with a series of black spots running through it. The body is generally smooth, free of both barnacles and callosities. The upper jaw is very narrow when viewed from above, and there is a prominent indentation behind the blowhole. There is no dorsal fin. The flippers are dark on both sides. There may be a pale gray ring around the tail stock. The flukes, which are up to 23 ft (7 m) wide, are also dark on both sides. The Bowhead's baleen is longer than that of any other whale—it is usually 10–13 ft (3–4 m) long, with a maximum recorded length of 17 ft (5.2 m)—and there is no baleen at the front of the mouth. Female Bowhead Whales are generally larger than males.

OTHER DISPLAYS: Before a dive, a Bowhead Whale may raise its tremendous flukes into the air. This whale also breaches occasionally, with half to three-quarters of its body leaving the water vertically and falling on one side with a tremendous splash.

GROUP SIZE: Bowheads are seen either singly or in small groups of up to six members. Good feeding sites may attract up to 15 whales. Rarely, during migration events, Bowheads may form loose groups of up to 60 individuals.

BLOW: This whale has widely separated blowholes. The resulting blow is broadly V-shaped, and it can rise up to 23 ft (7 m).

DIVE SEQUENCE

RANGE: The Bowhead Whale is found primarily in western arctic seas (whaling decimated its populations in the eastern Arctic). It has a short, nomadic migration that matches the advance and retreat of the sea ice.

STATUS: Endangered (USFWS/COSEWIC)

TOTAL LENGTH: up to 65 ft (20 m); average 57 ft (17 m)

TOTAL WEIGHT: up to 120 tons (109,000 kg); average 80 tons (73,000 kg)

BIRTH LENGTH: 12–15 ft (3.7–4.6 m)

BIRTH WEIGHT: unknown

FEEDING: Bowhead Whales are often seen skim-feeding through waters rich in krill and other copepods. Several whales may form a U-shaped group while skim-feeding in the same direction at the same speed.

REPRODUCTION: In summer, these whales are found in higher arctic seas, where they mate. Gestation is 13 months, and females give birth to one calf in August, alternating at least two years between pregnancies.

Calves nurse for about one year, and both sexes become sexually mature at 38–40 ft (12 m). Bowhead Whales are believed to live for over 200 years.

Northern Right Whale

SIMILAR SPECIES:
Northern Right Whale (p. 58).

Toothed Whales

BELUGA AND NARWAL FAMILY (MONODONTIDAE)

This small family of whales includes only the Beluga and the Narwhal, polar species that follow the seasonal formation and retreat of ice in the Arctic. These two whales are known to intermingle, and temporary nursery colonies have even formed with members from both species. Belugas are more widespread than Narwhals, and on the West Coast they can be found in both the Bering Sea and in the Gulf of Alaska. These whales do not have fused neck vertebrae—an unusual characteristic for cetaceans—and they are able to turn their heads, nod and look around in a manner unlike other whales.

Beluga

OCEAN DOLPHIN FAMILY (DELPHINIDAE)

This large family of toothed whales represents the true ocean dolphins, and it includes some of the most well-known cetaceans—aquariums, movies and anecdotal accounts have made Bottlenosed Dolphins and Orcas world-famous cetaceans. There are at least 33 delphinid species worldwide, but some evidence indicates that certain species, like the Bottlenosed Dolphin, may actually be two or three distinct species. At least nine species of delphinids exist in the waters of British Columbia and Alaska.

Pacific White-sided Dolphin

Although many people call the Orca a whale, it is actually the largest dolphin in the world. The Orca and its smaller relatives, such as the False Killer Whale and the pilot whales, are frequently referred to as "blackfish." Several authorities recognize these cetaceans as a separate family, but based on anatomical similarities, they are best classified as delphinids.

PORPOISE FAMILY (PHOCOENIDAE)

Porpoises, which number only six species worldwide, are widely distributed in the world, and there is very little range overlap between species. Although they superficially resemble dolphins, porpoises have unique features that set them apart from the better-known delphinids. They do not have a distinct beak, and their heads are quite rounded in appearance.

Dall's Porpoise

Their body shape is a bit more robust than the streamlined dolphins, and their flippers are typically small and stubby. Unlike dolphins, which have conical teeth for holding and biting prey, porpoises have flattened, spade-shaped teeth that function to slice their prey.

BEAKED WHALE FAMILY (ZIPHIIDAE)

Beaked whales represent a large but poorly understood family of whales. They mainly inhabit deep ocean waters where people rarely visit, so accounts of their habits and behavior are few. Some species of beaked whales have never been seen alive and are known only from individuals found dead on the shore or pulled in by fishing nets. There are 20 known species, but unrecorded beaked whale species may exist.

The ziphiids are referred to as beaked whales because all of them have a prominent snout. Males have two or four teeth that erupt on their lower jaw, either in the front or along the sides. Females and juveniles usually do not have erupted teeth of any sort. The lower jaws of the males and mature females may slope upward in the middle, giving the appearance that the "lip" is wrapping around the upper jaw. The teeth of the males further exaggerate this arch, and in some species the two teeth wrap over the upper jaw. This feature greatly reduces the ability of the whale to open its jaws, but beaked whales are believed to feed by sucking their prey into their mouths.

Stejneger's Beaked Whale

DWARF SPERM WHALE FAMILY (KOGIIDAE)
SPERM WHALE FAMILY (PHYSETERIDAE)

Two families worldwide represent the sperm whales. The famous Sperm Whale, subject of Herman Melville's book, *Moby Dick*, belongs to the family Physeteridae. The smaller sperm whales, in the family Kogiidae, are poorly understood and very little information exists about their habits and natural history.

The most distinguishing feature of a sperm whale is its extremely large head. The largest of all, the head of a male Sperm Whale may be as much as one-third of the length of its body. The exact function of the large head is still under much debate. Some people think its serves to focus the echolocation clicks when the whale searches for food in very deep and dark water. Other theories suggest that the head, full of high-quality spermaceti oil, controls the buoyancy of the whale as it rises and dives through the water.

Sperm Whale

Beluga

Delphinapterus leucas

In the far northern waters of the world, the elegant white Beluga thrives among the blue-white icebergs. This whale is unmistakable, but passing boats can overlook it amid the floating chunks of ice. Often nicknamed "sea canary" by sailors, this loquacious whale has a vast repertoire of whistles, warbles, squeaks, clucks and squeals unlike any other cetacean's in the world. A Beluga produces these sounds in the air passages in its head, and they are probably modified and amplified in the "melon," or forehead. Belugas seem to have the unique ability to bulge or shrink their melon at will, which may account for the large variety of sounds they produce.

The melon of the Beluga, like that of other toothed whales, functions primarily for sound amplification and detection for echolocation. Given the sophistication of the Beluga's melon, it probably has one of the best sonar systems of any whale. A Beluga can navigate in water that is barely deep enough to cover its body, as well as in open ocean.

Despite many research efforts, we do not know the significance of the Beluga's calls. We know that certain sounds are associated with courtship and familial greetings, but whether these whales just chatter noisily, or if they are actually communicating with language remains a mystery. In cases where a juvenile has stranded and must wait six hours for a new high tide—risking sunburn, dehydration and detection by a Polar Bear—the sounds made by the pod members in the water are distinctive. In one case where a stranded juvenile survived the tide and returned to the bay, the cacophony of squeaks and trills from its pod were distinctly different from their earlier sounds.

RANGE: The Beluga has a circumpolar distribution in the subarctic and High Arctic. Its movements follow the formation and retreat of seasonal ice.

OTHER NAMES: White Whale, Sea Canary

STATUS: Endangered (COSEWIC) in some areas; locally common in the subarctic

TOTAL LENGTH: up to 18 ft (5.5 m); average 13 ft (4 m)

TOTAL WEIGHT: up to 1.8 tons (1600 kg); average 1800 lb (820 kg)

BIRTH LENGTH: about 5 ft (1.5 m)

BIRTH WEIGHT: about 180 lb (82 kg)

TOOTHED WHALES

On the East Coast, an anomalous but stable population of Belugas survives in the St. Lawrence and Saguenay rivers. It is believed that these Belugas remained there after the northward retreat of sea ice following the last ice age. Although the population is stable, the whales may suffer ill-health from the terrible pollutants that contaminate their bodies. When the Belugas of the St. Lawrence die, their bodies must be removed and treated like toxic waste because of the toxins stored in their fat.

DESCRIPTION: An adult Beluga is unmistakable with its white body. It molts annually, and just prior to molting, its old skin appears yellow. After the molt, the new skin is gleaming white. A Beluga does not turn white until it is about five or six years old, and as a juvenile it is dark brown, slate blue or pinkish gray. The Beluga has a small, bulbous head with a very short but prominent beak. The flippers may curl upward slightly, and so may the tips of the flukes. The trailing edge of the flukes and the dorsal ridge may have a brown tinge. The flukes are notched in the middle and may appear convex in shape. Despite its robust appearance, the Beluga is an extremely flexible creature.

Its neck vertebrae are not fused like in most other whales, so it can move and nod its head around as it watches its surroundings. Its body is also flexible, and it can twist and turn as it dives underwater. Male Belugas are generally larger than females.

BLOW: The blow of the Beluga is low and steamy and can only be seen on calm, cool days. You may have more luck if you listen for the loud, puffing sound instead.

OTHER DISPLAYS: Belugas do not breach, but they frequently spy-hop and lob-tail. When they rise above the surface, they turn their heads left and right as they survey few thousand of these whales may gather together at river deltas.

FEEDING: The Beluga feeds on a variety of sea creatures, such as squid, fish, mollusks and other invertebrates. Although it may feed near the surface, it frequently dives deep into the ocean, sometimes to a depth of $1/2$ mi (800 m), where it is presumably feeding on deepwater creatures, such as squid.

REPRODUCTION: When a female is ready to give birth, she swims into deltaic calving waters that are one or two degrees warmer than the open sea. Nevertheless, the shock received to a newborn must be great, because it goes from a warm, environment inside its mother to the cold surrounding water. The calf stays with its mother for a least two years, and sometimes as long as four years if the mother does not get pregnant immediately after the calf is weaned. Normally, a female gives birth every two to three years. Peak calving period is in late summer, mating is in early spring or summer, and gestation is about 14 months. Males become sexually mature when they are at least eight years old and females when they are four to seven years old.

their surroundings. Because Belugas are gleaming white, their activities underwater are visible provided they are not too deep. When they are molting, they roll and rub themselves on the bottom. In shallow river deltas, where hundreds of Belugas can be seen together, their frolicking and playful behavior is visible. In many cases, Belugas underwater near a whale-watching boat will turn upside-down while swimming so they can look up at the human observers on the deck above them.

GROUP SIZE: Belugas are commonly seen in small groups of 5 to 20 members, but at certain times of the year hundreds or even a

Risso's Dolphin

SIMILAR SPECIES: Risso's Dolphin (p. 80).

Striped Dolphin

Stenella coeruleoalba

DESCRIPTION: This streamlined dolphin is easy to recognize because of the distinct, thin stripe running from its eye to the underside of its tail stock. The Striped Dolphin is gray over most of its back, light gray on its sides and white or pinkish underneath. The border between the dark and light gray colors forms a zigzag below the dorsal fin. The dorsal fin is curved, and both the fin and flippers are dark on both sides. The pale gray flukes are slightly concave and notched in the middle. The beak is prominent and darkly colored.

BLOW: This dolphin does not have a visible blow, but if you are close enough, the sound of its breath is audible.

OTHER DISPLAYS: The Striped Dolphin is highly acrobatic, and it breaches the water to heights up to 23 ft (7 m). It may turn somersaults in the air or turn tail spins, re-entering the water in a graceful dive. This dolphin can "porpoise" through the water upside-down.

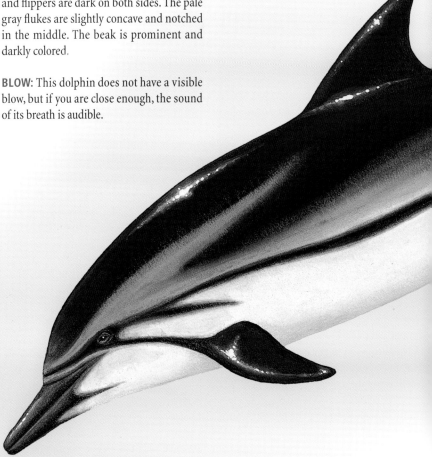

RANGE: Striped Dolphins can be found in warm-temperature, subtropical and tropical waters around the world.

STATUS: Locally common in some areas; insufficient data worldwide

TOTAL LENGTH: up to 9 ft (2.7 m); average 7 ft (2.1 m)

TOTAL WEIGHT: up to 350 lb (160 kg); average 260 lb (120 kg)

BIRTH LENGTH: 3–3½ ft (91–107 cm)

BIRTH WEIGHT: unknown

GROUP SIZE: Striped Dolphins are commonly found in herds of 100 to 500 members. In some circumstances, up to 3000 have been seen together.

FEEDING: This dolphin's primary diet is small to medium-sized fish and squid.

REPRODUCTION: Successful mating can occur in either summer or winter. After a gestation of 12 to 13 months, the female gives birth to one calf. Females are sexually mature at about 90 percent of their adult length. Males, although they are sexually mature when they are about 9 years old, are not socially mature enough to mate until they are 16 years old.

Saddleback Dolphin

SIMILAR SPECIES: Saddleback Dolphins (p. 72); Pacific White-sided Dolphin (p. 76).

Saddleback Dolphins

Delphinus spp.

More so than any other dolphins, the saddleback dolphins seem to confound both taxonomists and biologists alike. At least 20 species have been proposed worldwide, as well as several subspecies. Officially, the group was recently split into two species: the Short-beaked Saddleback Dolphin (*D. delphis*) and the Long-beaked Saddleback Dolphin (*D. capensis*). As the names suggest, the latter has a longer beak than the former, and, in general, the Long-beaked Saddleback Dolphin has a longer and slightly slimmer body, more muted coloration and a thicker dark line from the lower jaw to the flipper than the Short-beaked Saddleback Dolphin.

These key differences are often insufficient for an accurate identification, however, because there are many color and shape variations within each species. Even the sexes vary slightly in color and pattern. Because these two dolphins are so difficult to distin-guish in the wild, and considering their lengthy names, many people simply refer to them collectively as "saddleback dolphins." These two dolphins have such similar life histories and ranges that we have discussed them together here.

Like many other dolphins, saddleback dolphins are able to make an array of different sounds: they click, squeak and whistle, and they have a particularly high-pitched squeal that can even be heard from above the water. When large groups of saddleback dolphins are playing, they can be so loud and loquacious that they are heard long before they are seen. If the herd is startled, they bunch tightly together for safety.

RANGE: Saddleback dolphins are widely distributed in warm-temperate, subtropical and tropical waters of the world. In the Pacific Northwest, they are not likely to be found farther north than the southern tip of Vancouver Island.

OTHER NAMES: Common Dolphin, Criss-cross Dolphin

STATUS: Common

TOTAL LENGTH: up to 8½ ft (2.6 m); average 6½ ft (2 m)

TOTAL WEIGHT: up to 300 lb (140 kg); average 170 lb (77 kg)

BIRTH LENGTH: about 2½ ft (76 cm)

BIRTH WEIGHT: unknown

TOOTHED WHALES

Short-beaked Saddleback Dolphin

Saddleback dolphins are very wary of Orcas (p. 86) and sharks, and if the alarm is called they may retreat to lagoons or rough surf zones to avoid predators. Even when they are resting, they are alert for danger. Dolphins literally have the ability to sleep in halves: they are able to rest one eye while the other stays alert. Their brain also rests one hemisphere at a time, allowing for a constant state of awareness.

Unfortunately, one danger to which dolphins are oblivious is fishing nets, and a significant number of saddleback dolphins are killed each year by fishing activities. Saddleback dolphins may be at greater risk of getting caught in nets than other dolphins, because in some waters they associate closely with yellowfin tuna.

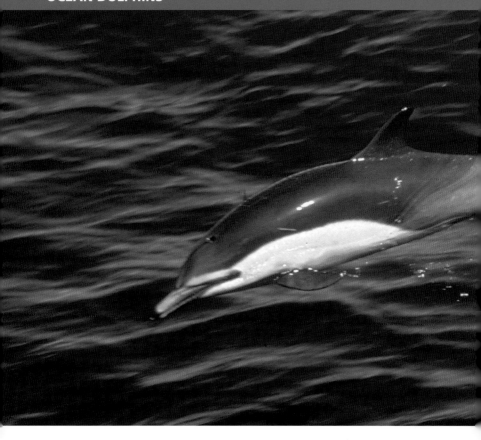

DESCRIPTION: This small to mid-sized dolphin is easy to identify because of its unique coloration. On its sides, beginning behind the eye, there is an arching, tan-colored patch. This patch can be quite yellowish or sometimes a dull muddy gray color. The tail stock is colored light gray, also in an arch, and where the gray meets the yellowish patch on the side, there is a distinct crisscrossing pattern. The back is mainly dark brown or bluish black, and the undersides are whitish. The beak is darkly colored and sometimes white-tipped, and there are streaks of white or gray around the face. A dark circle always surrounds the eye, and a dark streak runs from the lower jaw to the flipper. The broad flippers are dark on both sides, as are the pointed flukes. The triangular dorsal fin is centrally located, and often the center is lighter gray than the rim. The flippers, dorsal fin and flukes all trail backward, giving the dolphin a streamlined appearance.

Short-beaked
Saddleback Dolphin

Long-beaked
Saddleback Dolphin

of saddleback dolphins may be in the millions. Some groups as large as 2000 have been seen in warm waters, but a more typical group size is 10 to 500.

FEEDING: Saddleback dolphins feed mainly on small schooling fish, such as herring, anchovies and sardines. A group of dolphins typically herds the fish into a tight ball and then begins feeding. Such cooperative strategies are used by many species of dolphins. Feeding seabirds can attract dolphins to an area, because their flock usually indicates a sizable school of fish. Conversely, feeding dolphins can attract seabirds that benefit from the herded fish.

REPRODUCTION: The reproductive ages and lengths of saddleback dolphins can vary between different regions and subspecies, but generally females are sexually mature when they are 6 ft (1.8 m) long, and males when they are 6^1/$_2$ ft (2 m) long. Mating and calving can occur at any time of the year, and gestation is 11 to 12 months. The social structure of a group might influence courtship and mating.

BLOW: The blow of a saddleback dolphin is generally not visible. At close range, however, the sound of its breathing can be heard when it is in mid-leap.

OTHER DISPLAYS: Saddleback dolphins are exceptional acrobats, and they frolic and play in noisy displays. They may leap high out of the water and fall gracefully back in with little splash. They frequently bow-ride, and other displays include flipper slaps, chin slaps, lob-tailing and somersaults while breaching.

GROUP SIZE: Perhaps the most numerous dolphins in the world, the world population

Striped Dolphin

SIMILAR SPECIES: Striped Dolphin (p. 70); Pacific White-sided Dolphin (p. 76).

Pacific White-sided Dolphin

Lagenorhynchus obliquidens

Acrobatic Pacific White-sided Dolphins are favorites of whale watchers on the West Coast. These boisterous dolphins are so inquisitive and entertaining that they frequently "steal the show" from larger, less-engaging cetaceans. Do these dolphins enjoy entertaining? It would seem so, because they often increase their antics when boats full of eager whale watchers are around. On one occasion, to the astonishment of the viewers, an overly zealous individual leaped more than 10 ft (3 m) out of the water and accidentally landed on the deck of a large research boat. Of course, the exhibitionist was quickly returned to the water by the researchers, but the event remains a tribute to the impressive antics of these dolphins.

Pacific White-sided Dolphins and other members of the same genus are often referred to as "lags," a diminutive of their scientific name. As a group, these dolphins are not only acrobatic but very sociable as well. Together they surf ocean waves, catch wakes, ride bow waves and "porpoise" in unison. Sometimes, gatherings of 1000 or 2000 white-sided dolphins occur in offshore waters. They also socialize with other dolphins and marine mammals, most notably the Northern Right Whale Dolphin, seals and sea-lions.

Despite their gentle faces and social behavior, Pacific White-sided Dolphins can sometimes be pesky to larger whales, much like crows and magpies can be bothersome to your pet dog. White-sided dolphins have been seen clustering around the heads of Orcas (p. 86) and Humpbacks (p. 54) until the large whales get fed up and dive deep to get away.

RANGE: Pacific White-sided Dolphins are found only in the northern portion of the Pacific Ocean.

OTHER NAMES: Lag, Pacific Striped Dolphin, White-striped Dolphin, Hook-finned Dolphin

STATUS: Common

TOTAL LENGTH: up to 8 ft (2.4 m); average 7 ft (2.1 m)

TOTAL WEIGHT: up to 400 lb (180 kg); average 210 lb (95 kg)

BIRTH LENGTH: about 3 ft (91 cm)

BIRTH WEIGHT: about 30 lb (14 kg)

TOOTHED WHALES

Sometimes they can even be aggressive, both with other species of marine mammals and with each other.

Recently, the numbers of these dolphins have been increasing around Vancouver Island and in the region between the island and the mainland. No one can accurately explain this occurrence, because the species was previously thought to prefer the open ocean. Some interesting evidence shows that capelin, which reportedly smell like cucumbers, are now found in increasing numbers where previously there were none, and the white-sided dolphins appear to love eating these little fish.

Like most dolphins, Pacific White-sided Dolphins have acute senses that enable them to perceive their marine environment in an extremely sophisticated manner. Their sense of touch is many times greater than our own, and they can feel subtle changes in the pressure of the water around them. If another creature approaches a dolphin from behind its field of vision, the dolphin can

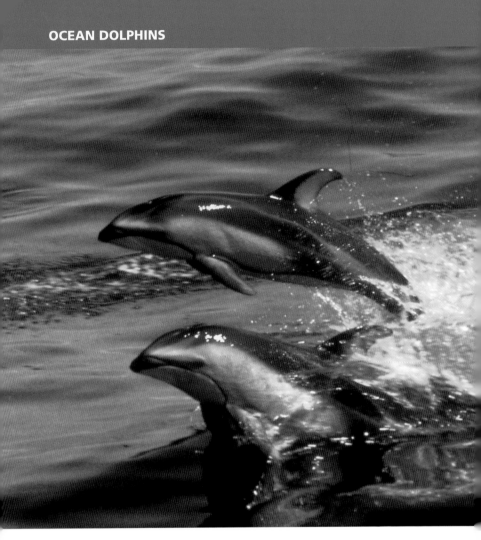

detect the animal's approach by the pressure wave displacement before it is seen or touched. This ability is undoubtedly advantageous at night and in deep water where light cannot penetrate.

Because their senses of touch and echolocation are so highly sophisticated, it is a common misconception that dolphins have poor eyesight. In fact, dolphins have exceptionally good eyesight both in and out of the water. When a dolphin leaps into the air, it is able to see all of its surroundings. A human, by comparison, is faced with blurry images if they take their goggles off in water—a medium that is about 800 times denser than air.

DESCRIPTION: The Pacific White-sided Dolphin has a distinct and beautiful color pattern of white, gray and nearly black. Its back is mainly dark, and beginning in front of the eye there is a large grayish patch that extends down the sides to below the dorsal fin. Along the sides of the tail stock there is

BLOW: White-sided dolphins do not make a distinct blow, but they often splash about and produce sprays that resemble a blow.

OTHER DISPLAYS: These acrobats perform virtually any kind of abovewater display, including dazzling breaches and somersaults. They often swim under the surface with just their dorsal fin exposed to slice and spray through the water.

GROUP SIZE: The Pacific White-sided Dolphin is commonly seen in groups of 10 to 50 members. Larger groups may sometimes form temporarily.

FEEDING: White-sided dolphins eat a variety of creatures, such as squid, anchovies, hake and other small fish. They feed in groups to better herd the fish, and each adult consumes about 20 lb (9 kg) a day.

REPRODUCTION: Calving and mating occur from late spring to fall, and gestation is estimated at 9 to 12 months. A mother nurses her calf for up to 18 months, and soon after weaning the female gives birth again. Both sexes reach sexual maturity when they are about 6 ft (1.8 m) long. Social maturity influences the age of first mating.

another similarly colored patch that may thin into a streak that runs forward of the dorsal fin. A distinct, dark lateral line borders the pure white undersides. The eyes are dark, as is the tip of its barely discernible beak. The most distinguishing feature is the rearward-pointing, bicolored dorsal fin, which is dark on the leading edge and pale gray on the trailing edge. The flippers may be similarly colored, but they are often dark all over. The flukes are pointed, slightly notched and dark on both sides.

Striped Dolphin

SIMILAR SPECIES: Striped Dolphin (p. 70); Saddleback Dolphins (p. 72); Harbor Porpoise (p. 92); Dall's Porpoise (p. 96).

Risso's Dolphin

Grampus griseus

DESCRIPTION: Unlike almost every other dolphin or whale in the world, the Risso's Dolphin becomes so heavily scarred that old individuals can appear almost white. The scars result either from teeth scratches incurred during sparring matches with each other or from squid bites. This dolphin is stout bodied and blunt headed. It has an unmistakably tall dorsal fin, long, sickle-shaped flippers and pointed, trailing flukes. Male Risso's Dolphins are generally larger than females.

BLOW: The Risso's Dolphin does not make a visible blow, but the sound of its breath is audible if the animal is close.

OTHER DISPLAYS: These dolphins are not as acrobatic as the smaller dolphins, but younger animals may breach fully out of the water. They are also seen spy-hopping, lob-tailing and flipper-slapping. Although Risso's Dolphins rarely bow-ride, they often surf in waves and wakes.

GROUP SIZE: Risso's Dolphins are regularly seen in groups of 3 to 50 individuals. Some groups can be as large as 150, and good feeding areas can attracted several hundred dolphins at one time.

FEEDING: In deep water, these agile dolphins feed primarily on squid, although some medium-sized fish are also eaten.

RANGE: Risso's Dolphins are found in deep, tropical and warm-temperate waters throughout the world. They avoid cold polar waters.

STATUS: Common

TOTAL LENGTH: up to 13 ft (4 m); average 10 ft (3 m)

TOTAL WEIGHT: up to 1100 lb (500 kg); average 880 lb (400 kg)

BIRTH LENGTH: 4–5½ ft (1.2–1.7 m)

BIRTH WEIGHT: unknown

TOOTHED WHALES

REPRODUCTION: Mating occurs primarily in spring, although the exact timing varies between different populations. Females give birth to one calf, usually in summer, after a gestation of 13 to 14 months. Both sexes are sexually mature when they are about 8½ ft (2.6 m) long.

Short-finned Pilot Whale

SIMILAR SPECIES: Beluga (p. 66); Short-finned Pilot Whale (p. 84).

False Killer Whale

Pseudorca crassidens

DESCRIPTION: The False Killer Whale is almost entirely black or deep gray, except for a light gray "W" or anchor-shaped patch on its undersides between the flippers. The snout is blunt and rounded, with the upper jaw protruding past the lower jaw. It has up to 24 teeth in each upper and lower jaw. The dorsal fin is upright, slightly rounded and located in the center of the dorsal line. The flippers appear slightly S-shaped because of the humped leading edge. The tail flukes are mildly pointed and notched in the middle. Male False Killer Whales are generally larger than females.

BLOW: Like most small whales, False Killer Whales make no visible blow.

OTHER DISPLAYS: When these whales surface, they often rise, or "porpoise," out of the water, exposing their flippers. Occasionally, they have their mouths open and show their teeth. False Killer Whales breach frequently and twist back into the water with a tremendous splash. They also bow-ride, wake-ride and even make acrobatic leaps clear out of the water.

GROUP SIZE: False Killer Whales are commonly seen in groups of 10 to 50 individuals. Gatherings of several hundred may occur throughout the year.

FEEDING: These fast whales feed mainly on squid and large fish, such as yellowfin tuna. They have been known to attack and kill other cetaceans, such as dolphins and even a Humpback Whale (p. 54).

RANGE: The False Killer Whale is found in the open ocean in tropical and warm-temperate waters. Some wanderers have been recorded as far north as Alaska.

OTHER NAMES: Pseudorca, False Pilot Whale, Blackfish

STATUS: Rare

TOTAL LENGTH: up to 20 ft (6.1 m); average 17 ft (5.2 m)

TOTAL WEIGHT: up to 2.2 tons (2,000 kg); average 1.6 tons (1500 kg)

BIRTH LENGTH: 5–6½ ft (1.5–2 m)

BIRTH WEIGHT: 180 lb (82 kg)

Short-finned Pilot Whale

REPRODUCTION: False Killer Whales mate successfully throughout the year. The gestation period is believed to be between 12 and 16 months. Males and females mature at roughly 80 percent of their adult body length.

SIMILAR SPECIES: Short-finned Pilot Whale (p. 84); Orca (p. 86).

Short-finned Pilot Whale

Globicephala macrorhynchus

DESCRIPTION: The Short-finned Pilot Whale is a small, black or dark gray whale. It has a bulbous head and an upward-slanting mouth, and some individuals have a light gray streak rising diagonally behind the eye. The dorsal fin is variable in shape, but it is usually arched strongly backward, with a rounded tip and a concave trailing edge. This whale has a light W-shaped patch on its underside between its flippers (see p. 82), and a light gray, oval patch on the underside forward of the tail stock. The flippers are pointed and strongly arched backward, and they are 14 to 19 percent of the body length. The flukes are also strongly pointed and notched in the middle. Short-finned Pilot Whales found in the Northern Hemisphere are typically larger than those in the Southern Hemisphere, and males are much larger than females.

BLOW: This whale makes a strong blow that is visible in calm weather.

OTHER DISPLAYS: The most commonly seen behavior of the Short-finned Pilot Whale is "logging," in which entire pods loll at the surface and are approachable by boats. This pilot whale rarely breaches, but it may be seen "porpoising," lob-tailing and spy-hopping.

GROUP SIZE: The typical group size is 10 to 30 individuals, although certain circumstances may attract several hundred pilot whales to one place.

FEEDING: The favorite foods of this whale are squid and octopus, although some large fish may be eaten.

RANGE: The Short-finned Pilot Whale is found in the open ocean in tropical and warm temperate waters. Some individuals have been recorded as far north as Alaska.

OTHER NAMES: Pothead Whale, Pacific Pilot Whale, Blackfish

STATUS: Common

TOTAL LENGTH: up to 23 ft (7 m); average 19 ft (5.8 m)

TOTAL WEIGHT: up to 4 tons (3600 kg); average 2.5 tons (2300 kg)

BIRTH LENGTH: 4½–6 ft (1.4–1.8 m)

BIRTH WEIGHT: 140 lb (64 kg)

REPRODUCTION: Length at sexually maturity varies greatly, but for females the range is 11–13 ft (3.4–4 m) and for males it is 14–18 ft (4.3–5.5 m). The timing of mating varies regionally, and it probably occurs throughout the year. Gestation is roughly 15 months, and females nurse their calves for nearly two years.

False Killer Whale

SIMILAR SPECIES: Risso's Dolphin (p. 80); False Killer Whale (p. 82).

Orca

Orcinus orca

The Orca, with its striking colors and intelligent eyes, has fascinated humans for centuries. Once revered by the indigenous peoples of North America, the Orca is now an icon for such things as biodiversity protection and contact with nonhuman intelligence. Images of this white-and-black giant can be found on everything from coffee cups to international conservation documents.

The Orca lives in every ocean of the world, from the cold polar seas to the warm equatorial waters, and it is one of the most widely distributed mammals on earth. Uncontested as the top predator in the oceans, the Orca feeds on a wider variety of creatures than any other whale. It is regarded as an intelligent yet fearsome creature—it is the lion that rules the seas.

Studies along the Pacific coast of North America indicate that there are three distinct forms of Orcas. The two more common groups are the "transients" and the "residents," and they are distinguishable by appearance and behavior. Transient Orcas tend to be larger, and they have taller, straighter dorsal fins than residents. The transients live in smaller pods, from one to seven individuals, and they have large home ranges, where as resident Orcas have small ranges and travel along predictable routes. Transients are more likely to feed on other sea mammals,

RANGE: The most widespread of all whales, Orcas are found in all oceans and seas.

OTHER NAMES: Killer Whale

STATUS: Vulnerable; locally stable in British Columbia and Alaska

TOTAL LENGTH: up to 32 ft (9.8 m); average 28 ft (8.5 m)

TOTAL WEIGHT: up to 11 tons (10,000 kg); average 7.5 tons (6800 kg)

BIRTH LENGTH: 6–8 ft (1.8–2.4 m)

BIRTH WEIGHT: about 400 lb (180 kg)

they dive for up to 15 minutes, they make erratic direction changes while traveling, and they do not vocalize as much as residents. Resident Orcas, on the other hand, feed mainly on fish, they are highly vocal, and they rarely dive for longer than three or four minutes.

Recently, a new class of Orcas has been identified. These "offshore" Orcas resemble the residents in appearance, but they usually live farther out at sea. Much more research is needed to accurately describe the offshore Orcas.

Unlike the rorqual whales, Orcas have never been hunted heavily by humans. Some hunting has occurred in the past several decades, but it has not threatened the total population. One form of hunting that has taken many Orcas and their close cousins, the Bottlenosed Dolphins, is live hunting, in which Orcas are taken from the wild and introduced into the world aquarium trade, where they are expected to learn and perform tricks for the public. These activities cause much controversy, mainly because many people consider cetaceans to be extremely intelligent animals and think that keeping them in a closed aquarium is unjust.

Male

Female

Much of what we have learned about cetacean intelligence and biology, however, comes from aquarium studies, and this knowledge helps us to better understand and protect whales in the wild.

DESCRIPTION: The Orca is unmistakable: its body is black, its undersides and lower jaw are white, there are white patches behind the eyes and on its sides, its large flippers are paddle-shaped, and its dorsal fin is tall and triangular. The shape and size of the dorsal fin varies between each whale and can be used by scientists and whale watchers to identify specific individuals. Each whale has a uniquely shaped dorsal fin, which often bears scars, and a uniquely shaped saddle patch. Old males may have fins as tall as 6 ft (1.8 m), and the fins of some old individuals

They are often seen breaching clear out of the water, lob-tailing, flipper-slapping, logging and spy-hopping. They may speed-swim, or "porpoise," with their entire body leaving the water at each breath. Subsurface beaches of rounded pebbles can attract many Orcas, which seem to enjoy rubbing their bodies on the smooth stones.

GROUP SIZE: Orcas travel in pods of 3 to 25 individuals. Some social gatherings may attract several pods at one time.

FEEDING: Orcas feed on a wider variety of animals than any other whale, partly because of their global distribution. Several hundred animal species are potential prey to these top predators of the sea, including, but not limited to, seals, other whales and dolphins, dugongs, fish, sea turtles and birds. Even land mammals may be eaten—there are records of pods killing and eating Moose and Caribou that swim across narrow channels and rivers in Canada and Alaska.

may be wavy when seen straight on. Females have smaller and more curved dorsal fins than males. Behind the dorsal fin there is often a gray or purplish "saddle." An Orca's eye is located below and in front of the white facial spot. The snout tapers to a rounded point. The flukes are dark on top and whitish below, and they have pointed tips, concave trailing edges and a distinct notch in the middle. Male Orcas are much larger than females.

REPRODUCTION: Mating occurs between individuals of a pod—Orcas rarely breed outside their social group. Males reach maturity when they are about 19 ft (5.8 m) long, and females when they are about 16 ft (4.9 m) long. Winter appears to be the peak calving period, and gestation is believed to be 12 to 16 months.

BLOW: In cool air, the Orca makes a low, bushy blow.

OTHER DISPLAYS: Orcas are extremely acrobatic whales for their size. They are inquisitive and often approach boats, apparently to get a better look at the humans on board.

False Killer Whale

SIMILAR SPECIES:
False Killer Whale (p. 82).

Northern Right Whale Dolphin

Lissodelphis borealis

DESCRIPTION: This unmistakable, torpedo-shaped dolphin is the only dolphin in the Northern Hemisphere that lacks a dorsal fin. It is named after the Northern Right Whale (p. 58), which also lacks a dorsal fin. This dolphin's head is narrow and its beak is pointed, with the lower jaw protruding. It has a distinctive, white "chin." The Northern Right Whale Dolphin is mainly black, dark slate gray or dark brown, and it has some white between the flippers, in the navel area and on the underside of the tail stock. The flippers are small and slender. The backward-pointing flukes are narrow, notched, dark on the dorsal side and white below.

BLOW: As with most dolphins, the blow may be audible but is not visible.

OTHER DISPLAYS: This dolphin is shy and easily startled, but in ideal circumstances it can be seen leaping clear of the water,

breaching, lob-tailing and side-slapping. In one long leap, it can cover up to 23 ft (7 m). When many of these dolphins are traveling together at high speed, the water's surface resembles rapidly boiling water.

GROUP SIZE: Groups of these dolphins number between 5 and 200 individuals, but some aggregations as large as 3000 have been observed.

FEEDING: The Northern Right Whale Dolphin feeds mainly on small and mid-sized fish or squid. It takes its prey at the surface or at mid-depths—it does not feed far below the surface.

RANGE: Northern Right Whale Dolphins are found only in the North Pacific between the western coast of North America and Japan.

OTHER NAMES: Pacific Right Whale Porpoise

STATUS: Probably common

TOTAL LENGTH: up to 10 ft (3 m); average 8 ft (2.4 m)

TOTAL WEIGHT: up to 250 lb (110 kg); average 180 lb (82 kg)

BIRTH LENGTH: 28–39 in (71–99 cm)

BIRTH WEIGHT: unknown

REPRODUCTION: Sexual maturity occurs when an individual is 70 to 75 percent of its adult body length, although social maturity may also be a factor in the onset of sexual activity. Little is known about the reproductive history of these dolphins, except that the peak calving time is in winter and early spring.

Striped Dolphin

SIMILAR SPECIES: Striped Dolphin (p. 70); Saddleback Dolphins (p. 72).

Harbor Porpoise

Phocoena phocoena

The little Harbor Porpoise is the most widespread member of its family. It favors coastal waters, such as estuaries, shallow bays and tidal channels, and in British Columbia it has even been seen inland in the Columbia River.

In the past, this porpoise was a familiar sight to boaters and sailors of coastal waters, but its population is declining. In some regions, alarming numbers of Harbor Porpoises have washed up either dead or dying. Although the reasons are not clear, many scientists suspect that high levels of toxins and pollutants impair the immune systems of these and other cetaceans, which makes them more susceptible to life-threatening diseases.

Drowning deaths are another main reason why Harbor Porpoises are declining. Because of this porpoise's feeding habits, it is frequently caught in bottom-set gill nets, a kind of net that hangs deep in the water like a curtain. Almost every kind of deep net can

RANGE: Harbor Porpoises are found in cold-temperate and subarctic waters of the Northern Hemisphere. They occur in coastal waters no deeper than 980 ft (300 m), but preferably no deeper than 660 ft (200 m).

OTHER NAMES: Common Porpoise, Puffing Porpoise

STATUS: Declining

TOTAL LENGTH: up to 6½ ft (2 m); average 5 ft (1.5 m)

TOTAL WEIGHT: up to 150 lb (68 kg); average 130 lb (59 kg)

BIRTH LENGTH: 26–35 in (66–89 cm)

BIRTH WEIGHT: about 11 lb (5 kg)

trap and drown a cetacean, but the most sinister are nets that have been thrown away or lost by fishermen. An untended net catches numerous cetaceans, sea turtles, fish and other sea creatures until it is so heavy that it sinks to the bottom.

The solution to this problem is not easy, but leading researchers have been working on ways to warn animals, particularly porpoises, where the nets are. Some sounds repulse Harbor Porpoises, and now a device called a "pinger" can be specially made and fitted to the nets. The pinger emits a sound that the porpoises do not like, resulting in the porpoises steering clear of the net. In the future, devices such as this may help save the lives of thousands of porpoises and other cetaceans.

DESCRIPTION: This small porpoise is the smallest cetacean in the Pacific Northwest. Its markings are not distinct, so the best way to identify it is by general body shape, behavior and the sound it makes to breathe. It is mainly dark or slate gray over the back, fading to white underneath. In some individuals the color change is gradual, while in others the change is well defined, especially on the tail stock. Even on one individual, the color pattern may not be the same from one side to the other. The face is small, the head tapers gently and the mouth angles slightly upward. This porpoise has black "lips," and one or two black streaks lead back to its all-black flippers. The dorsal fin and flukes are black as well, and the flukes are pointed slightly backward and are notched in the middle. Upon close examination, you can see little bumps, or tubercles, on the leading edge of the dorsal fin and flippers.

BLOW: Although Harbor Porpoises are difficult to observe because they rarely show much of themselves abovewater, they make a remarkable sound when they breathe.

silently and motionlessly just below the surface of the water. This behavior also occurs at night, and it probably helps them remain undetected by predators. On rare occasions, Harbor Porpoises have been seen bowriding. When they swim quickly they may "porpoise" in and out of the water.

GROUP SIZE: Harbor Porpoises usually live in small groups of two to five individuals. Some groups have up to 15 members, and good feeding waters can attract from 50 to several hundred porpoises.

FEEDING: Harbor Porpoises feed in midwater or on the bottom, and their main foods include small schooling fish, such as anchovies or herring. They rarely venture into water more than 660 ft (200 m) deep.

REPRODUCTION: Both male and female Harbor Porpoises mature sexually between the ages of three and four. Mating usually occurs in early summer, and calving is 11 months later. The newborns are dull brown in color, and for the first few hours they have birth lines or creases circumscribing their bodies. This species is not long-lived; most die before they are 10 years old.

When a Harbor Porpoise breaks the surface, it makes a quick sneezing sound, which has earned it the nickname "puffing porpoise."

OTHER DISPLAYS: Like other porpoises, the Harbor Porpoise shows little of itself abovewater. It rarely performs acrobatics like dolphins, and it is not as fast and active as the Dall's Porpoise (p. 96). Only its comical sneezing sound attracts the attention of whale watchers. Harbor Porpoises do not like intruders, however, and if they are uncomfortable and want to hide they will lie

Pacific White-sided Dolphin

SIMILAR SPECIES: Pacific White-sided Dolphin (p. 76).

Dall's Porpoise

Phocoenoides dalli

The second smallest cetacean in the Pacific Northwest, the Dall's Porpoise is a welcome sight for boaters and whale watchers. It is a high-speed swimmer that frequently provides hours of delight for human spectators. Fortunately, it is very tolerant of human company, and the approach of boats rarely startles it.

Despite being a porpoise, the Dall's Porpoise does not actually "porpoise" through the water like dolphins and other small cetaceans do. Instead, it surfaces only long enough for a quick breath. In doing so, it creates the distinctive conical splash of water that is typical of this species.

Dall's Porpoises appear to undergo short migrations in the Pacific Northwest. In summer, they tend to move northward; in winter they move farther south. There may also be some inshore-offshore migration, perhaps in response to food availability. In some years, for unexplained reasons, mass assemblies of a few thousand individuals have been monitored moving through passages near Alaska and northern British Columbia.

RANGE: Dall's Porpoises are found in the North Pacific between 30° N and 62° N, both close to land and in the open sea.

OTHER NAMES: Spray Porpoise, True's Porpoise, White-flanked Porpoise

STATUS: Common but declining

TOTAL LENGTH: up to 8 ft (2.4 m); average 6 ft (1.8 m)

TOTAL WEIGHT: up to 490 lb (220 kg); average 300 lb (140 kg)

BIRTH LENGTH: 2½–3 ft (76–91 cm)

BIRTH WEIGHT: unknown

Like all dolphins and porpoises, Dall's Porpoises have the ability to rest just half of their brain at a time, which allows them to keep a constant state of awareness to remain vigilant for dangers. The major natural enemies to Dall's Porpoises are Orcas (p. 86) and sharks.

Worldwide efforts to protect whales have had many admirable results. Unfortunately, the Dall's Porpoise is still being hunted on a massive scale. Several countries take a total of at least 14,000—and sometimes as many as 45,000—Dall's Porpoises each year. Moreover, several thousand more are accidentally killed in fishing nets. These numbers are extremely high, and it is likely that the total population cannot sustain such losses.

DESCRIPTION: Often mistaken for a baby Orca by boaters, the Dall's Porpoise is distinctly colored black and white. Its head is black and tapers to a narrow mouth. Its "lips" are usually black, but on some individuals they are white. The black body is extremely robust for its length. There is a large white patch on the belly and sides: on some individuals it stretches from in front of the flippers

Top view of tail

to the tail stock; on others it begins about one-third of the way down the body. The black, triangular dorsal fin has a hooked tip, and it is usually light gray or white on the trailing half. The small flippers lie close to the head, and they are dark black on both sides. When viewed from above, the tail is shaped like a wide gingko leaf, and it has a white or gray trailing edge.

BLOW: When breathing, this porpoise does not make a visible blow. As it swims and darts and zigzags about. It seems to love bow-riding, and it will zoom toward a fast-moving boat like a black-and-white torpedo. If a Dall's Porpoise comes to the bow of your boat, don't slow down for a better look, because it quickly loses interest in boats going slower than about 12 mph (19 km/h).

GROUP SIZE: Dall's Porpoises are commonly found in groups of 10 to 20 individuals, although meetings of hundreds or even thousands may occur in some waters.

FEEDING: The Dall's Porpoise feeds both at the surface and in deep water. Its primary foods include squid, lanternfish, hake, mackerel, capelin and other schooling fish. Its maximum feeding depth has been estimated at about 1600 ft (490 m). This porpoise has a high metabolic rate and requires large amounts of food at frequent intervals.

REPRODUCTION: Males reach sexual maturity when they are about 6 ft (1.8 m) long; females when they are 5^1/$_2$ ft (1.7 m) long. Observations indicate two peaks in calving, one in February-March and another in July-August. Peak mating must have a similar split, because the gestation period is about 11^1/$_2$ months.

breaks the surface, a V-shaped cone of water comes off its head. Many boaters look for this "rooster-tail" to locate the porpoises, because it can be seen from a great distance away, even though the porpoise itself is not visible.

OTHER DISPLAYS: The Dall's Porpoise is not acrobatic and does not leap out of the water. Nevertheless, it is exceptionally fast—it is often clocked at speeds of up to 35 mph (56 km/h)—and it even seems hyperactive as it

Pacific White-sided Dolphin

SIMILAR SPECIES: Pacific White-sided Dolphin (p. 76); newborn Orca (p. 86).

Baird's Beaked Whale

Berardius bairdii

DESCRIPTION: The largest of the beaked whales, the Baird's Beaked Whale has an elongated, spindle-shaped body. It is mainly slate gray or dark brownish in color, and it typically has many light-colored scars over its sides and back. There are variable light-colored blotches on its undersides. It has a very small, stubby dorsal fin set far back on the dorsal ridge. The small, rounded flippers are set close to the head. The flukes are also small, and they have almost straight trailing edges. The beak is distinct, with the lower jaw protruding. The four teeth of the lower jaw are visible even when the mouth is closed. The forehead has a prominent bulge, and the blowhole is indented. Female Baird's Beaked Whales are generally larger than males.

BLOW: This large whale makes a small, bushy blow that is sometimes visible.

OTHER DISPLAYS: A pod of Baird's Beaked Whales travels in synchrony, rising and blowing at the same time. When they surface to breathe, the blow is quick, and the blowhole disappears before the dorsal fin or hump emerges. On rare occasions, these whales are seen breaching, spy-hopping and lob-tailing.

GROUP SIZE: Baird's Beaked Whales are often seen in groups of 3 to 50 individuals. Large groups may temporarily break up into smaller pods and later rejoin.

RANGE: Baird's Beaked Whales are found in the North Pacific Ocean and the Japan, Okhotsk and Bering seas.

OTHER NAMES: Giant Bottlenosed Whale, North Pacific Great Bottlenosed Whale, Giant Four-toothed Whale, Northern Four-toothed Whale

STATUS: Probably common; insufficient data worldwide

TOTAL LENGTH: up to 42 ft (13 m); average 38 ft (12 m)

TOTAL WEIGHT: up to 15 tons (13,600 kg); average 12 tons (10,900 kg)

BIRTH LENGTH: 14–15 ft (4.3–4.6 m)

BIRTH WEIGHT: unknown

TOOTHED WHALES

FEEDING: Baird's Beaked Whales feed on bottom-dwelling creatures, such as skates, crustaceans and squid. They avoid deep oceans and favor areas above the continental shelf or around seamounts, where the bottom is accessible and food is more abundant.

REPRODUCTION: Both males and females are sexually mature at 80 to 85 percent of their adult length. Gestation is estimated to

be about 17 months, and the peak calving period is in March and April. Very little else is known about the mating habits of these whales.

SIMILAR SPECIES: The Baird's Beaked Whale is twice the size of other beaked whales in the region, so only a juvenile Baird's could be confused with another beaked whale.

Cuvier's Beaked Whale

Ziphius cavirostris

DESCRIPTION: This whale is medium-sized and its color is highly variable, including cream, beige, brown and purplish or reddish black. The color pattern is swirled and blotchy, and most individuals have spots and scars along their sides and undersides. The head is triangular, with an indistinct beak and two small teeth on the lower, protruding jaw. The flippers are small and set close to the head, while the dorsal fin is small and set close to the tail. The flukes are pointed, only slightly notched in the middle and broad— almost a quarter of the length of the body. Female Cuvier's Beaked Whales are generally larger than males.

BLOW: The blow is usually invisible, but it may be seen after a long dive. It is low and bushy, and it generally points forward and to the left.

OTHER DISPLAYS: This beaked whale breaches infrequently, rising vertically and completely out of the water and falling ungracefully back in. It usually avoid boats and whale watchers, but there are a few notable cases where inquisitive individuals have approached boats.

GROUP SIZE: When solitary Cuvier's Beaked Whales are seen, they are usually old males. Normally, these whales form groups of 2 to 10 members, but pods as large as 25 have been recorded.

FEEDING: Cuvier's Beaked Whales make deep dives of 20 to 40 minutes to feed on deep-sea fish and squid. They are rarely seen close to land.

RANGE: The Cuvier's Beaked Whale is found throughout the world, in all seas except the cold polar waters. It is the most widespread member of its family, and probably the most common.

OTHER NAMES: Goose-beaked Whale, Cuvier's Whale

STATUS: Insufficiently known

TOTAL LENGTH: up to 23 ft (7 m); average 20 ft (6.1 m)

TOTAL WEIGHT: up to 3.5 tons (3200 kg); average 2.5 tons (2300 kg)

BIRTH LENGTH: 6½–9½ ft (2–2.9 m)

BIRTH WEIGHT: about 550 lb (250 kg)

Stejneger's Beaked Whale

REPRODUCTION: Sexually maturity for both males and females is reached at about 75 percent of the adult length. The peak periods for mating and calving are unknown, because these whales are poorly understood in the wild.

SIMILAR SPECIES:
Stejneger's Beaked Whale (p. 106).

Hubbs's Beaked Whale

Mesoplodon carlhubbsi

DESCRIPTION: To quickly identify this whale at sea, a male must be seen, because males have distinct, white facial markings. The females are nondescript shades of gray, but the males have bulging white foreheads and stocky white beaks. Two massive teeth are visible on either side of the jaw, even if the mouth is closed. Many long scars and white spots are typically seen over the dark gray body. The flippers are small and set close to the head, and the dorsal fin is small, curved and sits about two-thirds of the way back along the dorsal ridge. The flukes are lighter below than above, and they are slightly pointed but rarely notched. Information about this species has been gathered from a few stranded individuals.

BLOW: This whale probably raises its head clear of the water to breathe, but no accurate data is known.

OTHER DISPLAYS: Although this whale probably partakes in abovewater displays, humans have not seen it enough to document its behavior.

GROUP SIZE: Only one positive sighting of this whale has been recorded, so the details of its group and social behavior remain a mystery.

FEEDING: Like many other members of this family, the Hubbs's Beaked Whale feeds on squid and deepwater fish.

RANGE: The Hubbs's Beaked Whale lives in the deep, open water of the North Pacific around Japan and the western coast of Canada and the United States.

OTHER NAMES: Arch-beaked Whale

STATUS: Insufficiently known

TOTAL LENGTH: up to 18 ft (5.5 m); average 17 ft (5.2 m)

TOTAL WEIGHT: up to 1.7 tons (1500 kg); average 1.3 tons (1200 kg)

BIRTH LENGTH: 7½–8½ ft (2.3–2.6 m)

BIRTH WEIGHT: unknown

Stejneger's Beaked Whale

REPRODUCTION: Because this whale is so infrequently encountered in the wild, virtually nothing is known about its reproduction or mating behavior. It is believed that calving occurs in mid-summer.

SIMILAR SPECIES:
Stejneger's Beaked Whale (p. 106).

Stejneger's Beaked Whale

Mesoplodon stejnegeri

DESCRIPTION: This dark gray or nearly black beaked whale has a pointed head without a distinct bulge on the forehead. Females and young, which are difficult to distinguish from each other, are uniformly dark gray, with paler undersides. Some juveniles may have light streaks in the neck region. Males have two prominent lower teeth and a distinct, pale gray beak and lower jaw. The erupted teeth on the male's lower jaw produce a strongly curved mouth line. These teeth may curve over the upper jaw on older individuals. The flippers are small and narrow, and the dorsal fin is small and triangular. The flukes are wide and triangular, with a nearly straight trailing edge.

BLOW: The Stejneger's Beaked Whale makes an inconspicuous, small blow. After a deep dive, its blow may be visible.

OTHER DISPLAYS: This whale is not very approachable, and it tends to vacate an area when boats are around. Its dive sequence involves a simple roll at the surface, exposing little of the body. Other displays have not been documented but probably occur infrequently.

GROUP SIZE: This whale commonly forms groups of two to five members. Some groups may have as many as 15 members.

RANGE: Stejneger's Beaked Whales can be found in cold and subarctic waters of the North Pacific and the Sea of Japan.

OTHER NAMES: Saber-toothed Whale, Bering Sea Beaked Whale, North Pacific Beaked Whale

STATUS: Insufficiently known, but very rare

TOTAL LENGTH: up to 17 ft (5.2 m); average 16 ft (4.9 m)

TOTAL WEIGHT: up to 1.3 tons (1200 kg); average 1.2 tons (1100 kg)

BIRTH LENGTH: about 5 ft (1.5 m)

BIRTH WEIGHT: unknown

REPRODUCTION: Nothing is known about the mating behavior and reproductive history of this whale.

Cuvier's Beaked Whale

FEEDING: The Stejneger's Beaked Whale probably feeds on deepwater fish and squid. When it dives for food, it first performs a series of five or six shallow dives and then one long, deep dive lasting up to 15 minutes.

SIMILAR SPECIES: Cuvier's Beaked Whale (p. 102); Hubbs's Beaked Whale (p. 104)

Dwarf Sperm Whale

Kogia simus

DESCRIPTION: This unusual whale resembles a slightly fat shark. Its snout is short and squarish, and its mouth is tiny and underslung. There is a white streak behind the eye that resembles the gill slit on a shark. Overall, the body is dark or bluish gray, with lighter undersides. The flippers are short and broad, and the dorsal fin is pointed and has a concave trailing edge. The flukes are broad, pointed and notched in the middle. The blowhole is set above the eye and slightly displaced to the left.

BLOW: The Dwarf Sperm Whale does not make a distinct blow.

OTHER DISPLAYS: When this whale rises to breathe, it does not roll forward into a dive like other whales. Instead, it takes a quick breath and then simply drops out of sight. It may be seen resting at the surface, and it occasionally breaches—rising vertically out of the water and splashing back haphazardly. When startled, it may release a cloud of dark intestinal fluid that presumably distracts an intruder while it dives. These clouds may also be released to confuse prey.

GROUP SIZE: Dwarf Sperm Whales travel alone or in pairs. On occasion, they have been seen in groups of up to 10 individuals.

FEEDING: This whale has a small mouth and presumably eats small creatures. Its primary foods are thought to be cuttlefish, squid and fish.

RANGE: Dwarf Sperm Whales can be seen in a number of locations throughout deep temperate, subtropical and tropical waters in both the Northern and Southern hemispheres. Their distribution is probably patchy rather than continuous.

STATUS: Insufficiently known; probably stable

TOTAL LENGTH: up to 9 ft (2.7 m); average 8 ft (2.4 m)

TOTAL WEIGHT: up to 610 lb (280 kg); average 450 lb (200 kg)

BIRTH LENGTH: about 39 in (1 m)

BIRTH WEIGHT: 90–110 lb (41–50 kg)

REPRODUCTION: The gestation period for this whale is about nine months, and calving is at its peak during the summer months. Both sexes reach maturity when they are 75 to 80 percent of their adult length.

Risso's Dolphin

SIMILAR SPECIES: Risso's Dolphin (p. 80).

Sperm Whale

Physeter macrocephalus

The famous Sperm Whale is a definite record-breaker in the world of mammals. It is easily the deepest-diving mammal on Earth, and it can hold its breath for more than two hours. Sperm Whales seem not to have a maximum diving depth, because greater and greater dives keep being recorded. The restricting factor appears to be the time without oxygen, rather than the enormous pressure on the body. At 10,500 ft (3200 m), which is believed to be the deepest recorded dive, the pressure on the body is a staggering 317 atmospheres, yet Sperm Whales are still able to function.

The Sperm Whale's biggest adaptation to surviving these pressures is that before it dives, it removes the air from its lungs to help minimize the difference in pressure between its body cavities and the surrounding water. Because the whale's body, like ours, is mainly water, it resists compression.

The mammoth head of the Sperm Whale is filled with very fine quality oil, called spermaceti, and it may function to regulate

DIVE SEQUENCE

RANGE: The Sperm Whale can be found in deep waters worldwide. Although it is widespread, its distribution is patchy.

OTHER NAMES: Cachalot, Anvil-headed Whale

STATUS: Endangered (USFWS); locally stable in some waters

TOTAL LENGTH: up to 69 ft (21 m); average 48 ft (15 m)

TOTAL WEIGHT: up to 58 tons (53,000 kg); average 35 tons (32,000 kg)

BIRTH LENGTH: about 13 ft (4 m)

BIRTH WEIGHT: about 1 ton (910 kg)

the whale's buoyancy as it dives and surfaces. The other proposed theory is that the spermaceti serves to magnify or focus the whale's sound emission during echolocation. Perhaps the spermaceti performs both of these functions for the whale. Females have dramatically smaller heads than males, but the reason for this difference is not clearly understood. Females also dive deeply and rely on echolocation, so perhaps the larger head of the male serves another purpose.

DESCRIPTION: The Sperm Whale is easy to recognize because of its extremely large head and distinctive features. The head is as much as one-third of the total body length. It is narrow when seen from above and rectangular when seen from the side. A male has a much larger and more rectangular head than a female. The eyes are relatively small and inconspicuous. The mouth and tip of the snout may be white or light gray, and scarring may be obvious. The blowhole is slightly raised at the end of the snout, and it is displaced to the left. The overall body color is brown, gray or nearly black, although the undersides are often lighter. The stubby flippers and broad, triangular tail flukes are dark on both sides, but scarring may lighten the edges. The trailing edge of the flukes is sometimes scalloped, and such variations in the tail are used by researchers to identify individuals. Instead of a true dorsal fin, the Sperm Whale has a distinct hump or knuckle where the fin should be. Several smaller knuckles continue down the dorsal ridge to the tail. The skin appears "pruney" from behind the eye to the tail stock. Male Sperm Whales are much larger than females.

BLOW: Because the blowhole of the Sperm Whale is at the tip of the snout and displaced to the left, the blow sprays forward and to the left. No other whale makes a blow like this, so even from afar a Sperm Whale can be identified.

OTHER DISPLAYS: Sperm Whales may breach and lob-tail, especially juveniles.

dives is from two Sperm Whales that were believed to reach 10,500 ft (3200 m), where they consumed bottom-dwelling sharks. The main foods eaten by Sperm Whales are squid and Giant Squid, octopus, large fish and sharks. Sperm Whales locate their food in the darkness of deep water by using their extremely sophisticated echolocation.

REPRODUCTION: Although males are sexually mature when they are about 10 years old, they are unlikely to mate for several more years. Females are sexually mature when they are 8 to 12 years old. Mating usually occurs in late winter or early spring, and single calves are born in summer or fall, following a gestation of 14 to 15 months. The young may nurse for several years, even after they start eating solid food.

When they return from a deep dive, they breathe at the surface 30 or 40 times before diving again. The first breath is very loud and explosive, while the subsequent breaths are quieter. Between dives, the whales usually stay at the surface for about 15 minutes, but sometimes they will remain near the surface for as long as an hour.

GROUP SIZE: Sperm Whales usually live in groups of 2 to 25 animals. Nursery colonies of females and young number 12 to 30 individuals, and bachelor colonies of many young males are also common. At times, assemblages of hundreds or even thousands of Sperm Whales have been reported.

FEEDING: The ability of the Sperm Whale to feed at great depths is unsurpassed by any other mammal. One of the deepest recorded

Humpback Whale

SIMILAR SPECIES: Humpback Whale (p. 54), during the dive sequence.

Seals and Otters

During a trip on the waters off British Columbia and Alaska, you may see several mammals other than whales, including seals, sea-lions, walruses and otters. Although these other marine mammals are highly adapted to life in the ocean, unlike whales, they are able to come ashore at any time. All seals, sea-lions, walruses and otters are members of the order Carnivora, which also includes dogs, cats, bears and weasels, among others.

Outwardly, all the seals look similar, and they were once classified in their own order, Pinnipedia, meaning "fin feet." Further study revealed that seal-like mammals are actually a good example of convergent evolution, where creatures of different origins look or function similarly because of comparable adaptations to a common problem. There are two distinct lineages of seals: the eared seals (and their later offshoot, the Walrus) likely share a common ancestor with bears; the hair seals are descendants of an ancestral member of the weasel family. Despite having different lineages, all seals and sea-lions are still frequently referred to as pinnipeds.

EARED SEAL FAMILY (OTARIIDAE)

This family, which is found almost worldwide, includes the fur seals and the sea-lions. At a glance, it should be easy to tell this family of seals from the hair seals: all the eared seals have small but noticeable external ears, whereas the hair seals do not. As well, the eared seals can rotate their hindlimbs forward into a more leg-like position, which enables them to walk or even lope when on shore. Another good way to identify members of this family is that none of them has distinct markings on its fur. Although their coats may vary in color from light to dark brown or gray, there are no rings, spots or patterns. Eared seals have large, thick, hairless flippers with well-developed claws on the middle three digits of the hind flippers.

Northern Sea-Lion

Walrus

WALRUS FAMILY (ODOBENIDAE)

The Walrus—the only member of this family—is an unmistakable inhabitant of cold, polar and subpolar waters. Like the eared seals, the Walrus is able to rotate its hindlimbs under its body to help it move on land. Unlike most other seals, the Walrus spends much of the day hauled out on rocky shores or ice packs. The Walrus has two features that are similar to the hair seals: all of its digits have claws and it has no external ears. Perhaps the most distinguishing feature of the Walrus is its tusks. Both sexes have tusks, although they tend to be longer in males—male Pacific Walruses can have tusks reaching an astonishing 40 in (1 m) in length.

HAIR SEAL FAMILY (PHOCIDAE)

The hair seals are also referred to as either the earless seals or the "true" seals. As the former name suggests, they have no visible external ears. The best way to distinguish these seals from the eared seals, however, is by body shape. The hind flippers of hair seals are permanently pointed backward—these seals are unable to rotate their hindlimbs forward to help support their body weight when they are on land. As a result, on land hair seals move with clumsy undulations of their bodies. Whenever possible, such as on ice or snow, they slide or roll. Once in the water, hair seals are graceful, lithe swimmers capable of high speeds and rapid turns. Their forelimbs are small compared to those of eared seals, but the flippers are strong enough that the seal can hold itself upright and tread water at the surface. Members of this family all have hair on their flippers and claws on all five digits of each flipper.

Ribbon Seal

OTTER SUBFAMILY (LUTRINAE)

Otters are a subgroup of the weasel family (Mustelidae), which also includes terrestrial carnivores, such as minks, weasels, badgers and martens. There are two otters in North America: the Sea Otter and the Northern River Otter. The Sea Otter, which can be seen along the coasts of British Columbia and southern Alaska, spends almost its entire life in the water. It mates in the water, and females give birth and nurse their young in the water. Sea Otters typically only come ashore to wait out bad storms. The Northern River Otter is similar to the Sea Otter, except that it is smaller, slimmer and has a longer tail. Although the Northern River Otter inhabits inland freshwater and is not strictly a marine mammal, it is seen on the coast more often than the Sea Otter.

Sea Otter

Northern Fur Seal

Callorhinus ursinus

DESCRIPTION: The Northern Fur Seal has a small head, a short, pointed nose with long whiskers, small ears, large eyes and a very short tail. The front flippers are extremely large compared to the size of the body. When this seal is wet it looks sleek and black; when dry, males are mostly dark grayish black, while females show a brownish throat and often some silvery gray underparts. Adult males have a thickened neck and are more than twice the weight of females. Newborn pups are black.

RANGE: This wide-ranging species may undergo annual migrations of up to 6200 mi (10,000 km). It is found from California up the West Coast and across the North Pacific to Japan.

STATUS: Declining

TOTAL LENGTH: male 6–7½ ft (1.8–2.3 m); female 3½–5 ft (1.1–1.5 m)

TAIL LENGTH: 2 in (5.1 cm)

TOTAL WEIGHT: male 330–620 lb (150–280 kg); female 85–120 lb (39–54 kg)

SEALS & OTTERS

HABITAT: This seal is pelagic for 7 to 10 months of the year. It rests at sea by floating on its back, with its hind flippers bent up and laid onto its belly and held down by the fore flippers. It comes ashore only to breed, mainly on rocky beaches of the Pribilof and Commander islands.

FEEDING: Northern Fur Seals feed mainly on squid, herring, capelin and pollack up to 10 in (25 cm) long. Almost all feeding activity occurs at night.

REPRODUCTION: Males come ashore in late May and June and battle to establish their territories. Females come ashore in mid-June or July, and within two days they give birth to a pup that was conceived the previous summer. Mating occurs 8 to 10 days after the pup is born. The pup nurses for only four or five months.

Harbor Seal

SIMILAR SPECIES: Harbor Seal (p. 128); Northern Sea-Lion (p. 118)

Northern Sea-Lion

Eumetopias jubatus

The large Northern Sea-Lion is a familiar sight to many people who frequent coastal waters. It may be seen basking on shore or resting in the water in a vertical position, with its head above the surface. This pinniped is quite gregarious—it is usually seen in groups numbering a few hundred to thousands of individuals—and its social system is more advanced than that of the Harbor Seal (p. 128), which is another common West Coast pinniped. For example, when a group of sea-lions is feeding, they all dive at the same time and all surface together, which means that no one sea-lion dives first and scares the fish away, ruining the feeding opportunities for the others.

There is great sexual dimorphism in sea-lions, and males are three to four times as heavy as females—adult male Northern Sea-Lions are the largest of the eared seals. A large difference in weight is characteristic of seals with territorial males that hold a harem. Females form loose aggregations with their pups within a male's territory, and they are far faster and more agile than the males.

During the breeding and pupping season, hundreds of sea-lions congregate at rookery sites used by

RANGE: Northern Sea-Lions are found near the shore from southern California up to Alaska, through the Aleutian Islands to Siberia and south to Japan.

OTHER NAMES: Steller Sea-Lion

STATUS: Declining; endangered (USFWS) in some parts of its range

TOTAL LENGTH: male 8½–11 ft (2.6–3.4 m); female 6–7 ft (1.8–2.1 m)

TOTAL WEIGHT: male up to 2200 lb (1000 kg); female 600–800 lb (270–360 kg)

SEALS & OTTERS

generations of sea-lions. Mature bulls make a roaring sound at this time, and, when combined with the grumbles and growls of other colony members, the resulting cacophony can be heard for more than ½ mi (800 m). Adult males evicted from the breeding colony often bear huge cuts and tears on the neck and chest—reminders of the vicious battles waged over a territory.

Two major rookeries exist in British Columbia: one on the northwestern tip of Vancouver Island; the other near the southern end of the Queen Charlotte Islands. Outside the pupping season, the "bachelors," the young of that year, some

barren cows and the odd mature bull form loose colonies.

The Northern Sea-Lion is well noted for its exceptional curiosity and playfulness. It sometimes leaps clear from the water—it has even been seen jumping across surfaced whales—and it occasionally throws rocks back and forth. The smaller California Sea-Lion (p. 122), which shares this playfulness, is commonly seen performing tricks in marine park shows.

For many years, sea-lions were killed because it was believed that they fed on commercially valuable fish. Recent research indicates that they feed opportunistically on any available fish; common prey include octopus, squid and "scrap" fish, such as herring and greenling. Although the intentional killing of sea-lions has decreased, their populations have continued to decline by as much as 80 percent from historic numbers. The causes of this decline are unknown.

A unique characteristic of sea-lions is that they frequently swallow rocks as large as 5 in (13 cm) across. Although no one

knows for sure, the most likely explanation is that the stones help pulverize food inside a sea-lion's stomach. A sea-lion's teeth are ill-suited to chewing, and it regularly swallows large chunks of meat and whole fish.

DESCRIPTION: Adults are light buff to reddish brown when dry, and brown to nearly black when wet. Males, which are much larger than females, develop a huge neck that supports a mane of long, coarse hair. Females are sleek. The hind flippers can be drawn forward under the body, and, like all eared seals, sea-lions can jump and clamber up steep rocky slopes at an amazing rate. The fore flippers are strong and are used for propulsion underwater.

HABITAT: Northern Sea-Lions live mainly in coastal waters near rocky shores. They are seldom found more than 150 ft (46 m) from water, and they prefer to stay in the ocean during inclement weather. When it is sunny, they usually haul out and bask on rocky shores. They are known to swim up major rivers in search of lamprey and salmon.

FEEDING: These sea-lions feed primarily on fish, such as blackfish, greenling, rockfish and herring. Others foods include squid, octopus, shrimp, clams, salmon and bottom fish. Male sea-lions do not eat for one to two months while they are defending a territory.

REPRODUCTION: Males come ashore in early May and battle to establish their territories on rocky, boulder-strewn beaches or rock ledges. Females come ashore in mid-May or June, and within three days they give birth to a pup conceived during the previous summer. Mating occurs within two weeks after the pup is born. The pup typically nurses for about one year, but some have been known to nurse for as long as three years. Females may live to be 30 years old and are sexually mature at three to seven years. Males probably do not breed before age 10.

California Sea-Lion

SIMILAR SPECIES: California Sea-Lion (p. 122); Northern Elephant Seal (p. 144); Northern Fur Seal (p. 116).

California Sea-Lion

Zalophus californianus

DESCRIPTION: The California Sea-Lion has an elongated, slender body, a blunt snout and a short but distinct tail. Adult males are brown, and they develop a noticeably raised forehead that helps distinguish them from male Northern Sea-Lions (p. 118). Females are generally tan, with a slightly darker chest and abdomen. The coarse guard hairs of the coat cover only a small amount of underfur. The front flippers are long and bear distinct claws. California Sea-Lions are a noisy bunch—the males produce a honking bark, the cows wail and the pups bleat.

RANGE: The California Sea-Lion inhabits coastal waters of the North Pacific from Mexico to Vancouver Island. There are three small, isolated populations in the Sea of Japan.

STATUS: Vulnerable and declining

TOTAL LENGTH: male 6½–8 ft (2–2.4 m); female 4½–6½ ft (1.4–2 m)

TOTAL WEIGHT: male 440–860 lb (200–390 kg); female 100–250 lb (45–110 kg)

HABITAT: California Sea-Lions are normally seen in coastal waters around islands with rocky or sandy beaches. Preferred haul-out sites include sandy or boulder-strewn beaches below rocky cliffs. In some places they occupy sea caverns. They tend to avoid the rocky islets preferred by Northern Sea-Lions.

FEEDING: These sea-lions eat a wide variety of foods, including at least 50 species of fish and many types of squid, octopus and other mollusks.

REPRODUCTION: Males establish their territories on rocky or sandy beaches in May, June or July. Females arrive on the breeding grounds in May or June. If a female conceived the previous year, she will give birth to a pup, and within one month she mates again. Most pups are weaned by eight months, but a few may nurse for a year or more. They start eating fish before they are weaned.

Northern Sea-Lion

SIMILAR SPECIES: Northern Sea-Lion (p. 118); Northern Fur Seal (p. 116).

Walrus

Odobenus rosmarus

Truly one of a kind, the Walrus is the sole member of its family. It most likely arose from an ancestral eared seal, but after 7 million years of adaptation, the Walrus is unlike any other living seal. The Walrus's unique tusks, which grow throughout an individual's life, are its most distinguishing feature. The tusks are modified teeth, and they are coated in enamel when they first erupt. Over time, the enamel wears off, leaving a tusk of pure ivory.

The exploitation of Walruses for their ivory was once extensive, but it has nearly been stopped now, thanks to the Marine Mammal Protection Act. This 1972 U.S.

RANGE: The Pacific race of the Walrus is found from northeastern Siberia around Alaska to the Bering Sea.

STATUS: Stable

TOTAL LENGTH: male up to 12 ft (3.7 m); female up to 9½ ft (2.9 m)

WEIGHT: male up to 1.7 tons (1500 kg); female up to 1 ton (910 kg)

TUSK LENGTH: male up to 40 in (1 m); female up to 14 in (36 cm)

act protects Walruses and other marine mammals from game hunting and exploitation. Only the Inuit, who have traditional links to this animal, continue to hunt the Walrus. The Inuit use all parts of the animal: the meat is eaten; the bones become tools; the skin becomes leather for clothing or covers for boats; the blubber is used for oil and fuel; the intestines are used to make waterproof containers; the tusks are used as sled runners or for ornamentation. Recently, the Inuit have made ivory carvings to bring additional revenue into their communities.

There are two distinct Walrus races: the Pacific Walrus, which is the larger of the two, inhabits the region from the Chukchi Sea off northeastern Siberia to Alaska; the Atlantic Walrus lives in the Hudson Bay and east to Greenland. Both races of Walrus live in groups of anywhere from a few dozen to up to 2000 individuals.

The Pacific Walrus spends its summers closer to Siberia and winters near Alaska. When it migrates, it may swim, but it usually rides on ice packs moving with the ocean currents. When a Walrus's ice pack starts heading in the wrong direction, it dives off and swims to the next one going its way. The smaller Atlantic Walrus is not migratory, and it prefers landfast ice that does not travel.

Walruses are excellent swimmers that can reach speeds up to 15 mph (24 km/h). They may sleep on land, but they have the ability to sleep vertically in the water with their heads held up by inflated air sacs in the neck. When they dive for food, they can descend to 300 ft (91 m) deep, remaining underwater for as long as 30 minutes.

DESCRIPTION: Both bull and cow Walruses have tusks, but a cow's tusks are considerably shorter and more curled than a bull's. Walruses have very little hair over their bodies, and their skin color varies from pale pink, yellow, reddish or brownish to nearly white. The hind flippers have nails on all five digits and can be rotated underneath so the walrus can "walk" on all fours on land. The fore flippers lack nails completely. The face is covered with about 400 whiskers, each up to 12 in (30 cm) in length. Walruses have no visible tail.

HABITAT: Historically, Walruses may have inhabited more of the northern islands and rocky shores than they do now, but the impact of human hunting has pushed them farther into the arctic seas. Currently, they spend most of their time on pack ice over water that is usually about 60 ft (18 m) deep. Walruses spend more of their time basking than do other seals, usually on ice or rocky outcroppings.

FEEDING: Using its mouth like a powerful vacuum, the Walrus sucks mollusks out of their shells. Clams are the most common food, and a Walrus can polish off up to 6000 of these bivalves in one day. The Walrus is opportunistic, and it will feed on fish, crabs, shrimp, worms and a variety of other marine creatures.

REPRODUCTION: Unlike other seals that usually mate each year, a female Walrus mates once every two years. Gestation is 11 to 12 months, and the single newborn calf weighs 100–150 lb (45–68 kg). The cow nurses her calf in the water in a vertical position. The calf remains with the mother and nurses from her for nearly two years. The mother separates from the calf before she has another baby.

Northern Elephant Seal

SIMILAR SPECIES:
Northern Elephant Seal (p. 144).

Harbor Seal

Phoca vitulina

The inquisitive Harbor Seal is a well-known resident of the West Coast. This seal bespeckles the rocky coastline at almost any time of the day throughout the year. It basks on shore either alone or in groups numbering up to the thousands.

Although many Harbor Seals may bask on rocks together, they pay very little attention to their neighbors and seldom interact. Only during the pupping season is there interaction, and it is primarily between the females. Females with newborn pups may congregate in a "nursery" in shallow water where the pups can sleep. The pups and the females sleep underwater, rising occasionally for a breath. These nursery groups are not interactive, however, but simply a precautionary measure against predators—while most of the females and pups are sleeping, some are likely to be awake and watchful for danger. The same is true for hauled-out seals. Where several seals are together, the chances are good that there is always at least one individual awake and wary of approaching danger.

Harbor Seals tend to be cautious of humans, and if you approach them on land they are likely to dive immediately into the

RANGE: Harbor Seals are found along the northern coasts of North America, Europe and Asia. They inhabit the entire coast of British Columbia and Alaska.

STATUS: Common

TOTAL LENGTH: 4–6 ft (1.2–1.8 m)

TAIL LENGTH: 3½ - 4½ in (9–11cm)

TOTAL WEIGHT: 110–310 lb (50–140 kg)

SEALS & OTTERS

water. Many kayakers and boaters, however, have enjoyed watching inquisitive individuals that approach their boats for a better look. This kind of encounter is controlled by the seal: if it wants to see you, it will come closer; if it is afraid of you, it will leave. Do not approach a seal that has tried to flee you, because it can cause unnecessary stress on the animal.

When the tide is out at night, Harbor Seals sleep high and dry at favorite haul-out sites. They frequently rest with their heads and rear flippers lifted above the rock. During the day, they can sleep underwater in shallow coastal water by resting vertically just above the bottom. Young pups commonly rest in this manner. Harbor Seals can go without breathing for nearly 30 minutes, and although they sometimes wake up to breathe, they frequently rise to the surface, take a breath and then sink back to the bottom without waking. Harbor Seals are unable to sleep at the surface like sea-lions and sea otters can.

DESCRIPTION: The Harbor Seal is typically dark gray or brownish gray with light, blotchy spots or rings, but individuals may have the reverse color pattern—light gray or nearly white with dark spots. The undersides are generally lighter than the back. The outer coat is composed of stiff guard hairs about 3/8 in (1 cm) long, which is the characteristic that gives seals of this family the name "hair seals." The guard hairs cover an undercoat of sparse, curly hair, about 1/4 in (6 mm) long, that helps provide insulation for the seal. Pups bear a spotted, silvery or gray-brown coat at birth. The head is large, round and very dog-like, except that there are no visible ears. Each of the short front flippers has long, narrow claws. Male Harbor Seals are generally larger than females.

HABITAT: This near-shore seal is frequently found in bays and estuaries. Favored haul-out sites, which are traditionally used by many generations of Harbor Seals, commonly include intertidal sandbars, rocks and octopus, and crustaceans, such as crabs, shrimp and crayfish. Newly weaned pups seem to consume more shrimp and mollusks than do adults. Adult Harbor Seals have been seen taking fish from nets, and some have even entered fish traps to feed and then easily departed.

REPRODUCTION: The breeding season for Harbor Seals varies geographically. The farther north a population is located, the later its breeding and pupping occurs. Gestation lasts 10 months, and a single pup is born between April and August. The pups are weaned when they are four to six weeks old, after they have tripled their birth weight on their mother's milk, which is more than 50 percent fat. Within a few days of weaning her pup, a female mates again. Harbor Seals become sexually mature anywhere from three to seven years of age. Captive seals have lived more than 35 years, although the typical lifespan for males is 20 years and for females is 30 years.

rocky shores. The Harbor Seal sometimes follows fish several hundred miles up major rivers, and there are even permanent populations in some inland lakes. A famous resident population lives in Harrison Lake, British Columbia, more than 110 mi (180 km) upriver from the coast.

FEEDING: Harbor Seals feed primarily on fish, such as rockfish, cod, herring, flounder and salmon. To a lesser extent, they also feed on mollusks, such as clams, squid and

Northern Fur Seal

SIMILAR SPECIES: Northern Fur Seal (p. 116); Northern Sea-Lion (p. 118); Northern Elephant Seal (p. 144).

Spotted Seal

Phoca largha

DESCRIPTION: The Spotted Seal is usually gray with a silvery sheen on its sides, but it may range from brownish yellow to very dark gray. It gets its name from the many dark spots over its body, concentrated on the sides and back. Its undersides are usually cream colored and lightly spotted. The hind flippers are permanently oriented backward—they cannot be brought under the body to support its weight on shore. Male Spotted Seals are generally larger than females.

HABITAT: Spotted Seals are found in the cold waters of the Bering Sea. They haul out onto ice to rest and to give birth. Individual seals may have favorite haul-out sites.

FEEDING: Spotted Seals feed mainly on crustaceans and octopus, but fish, such as pollack, cod, capelin, herring and smelt, are also eaten. These seals are accomplished divers: adults can dive as deep as 1000 ft (300 m), and just a month after weaning the young can dive as deep as 250 ft (76 m).

RANGE: Spotted Seals live at the southern end of polar pack ice in the Bering Sea from Alaska to Siberia.

STATUS: Common

TOTAL LENGTH: 5–5½ ft (1.5–1.7 m)

TOTAL WEIGHT: 180–270 lb (82–120 kg)

SEALS & OTTERS

REPRODUCTION: Spotted Seals are annually monogamous: they pair off each year in April about 10 days before the female gives birth to a pup conceived the previous year. The pup is covered in white "lanugo" fur that it loses before it is weaned. Pups are weaned at one month, and shortly afterward the mother mates with the bull accompanying her. Once a pup starts swimming, it is abandoned by its mother.

Harbor Seal

SIMILAR SPECIES: Harbor Seal (p. 128).

Ringed Seal

Pusa hispida

Studies of the Ringed Seal have provided information not only about the biology of this small seal, but also about the biogeological history of the continent. By identifying the variety of sea creatures on which Ringed Seals feed, the faunal picture of the northern seas can be partially described, both in modern times and historically.

Fossils of Ringed Seals that have been discovered, some near Ottawa, give clues to the geology and habitat of an area more than 10,000 years ago. Both Ringed Seals and the shelled animals found with them are known to live in cold, saltwater habitats, so we can infer that similar conditions existed at one time where these fossils were found. More importantly, we know that other animals— the prey species of Ringed Seals—must have also lived in the region. In this way, the fossil history of the Ringed Seal can provide good information about our continent since the last ice age.

When a Ringed Seal dives for crustaceans, it can reach a maximum depth of about 300 ft (91 m). It can stay under for up to 18 minutes, although a dive usually lasts for 5 minutes or less. Unlike its cousin the Bearded Seal (p. 140), the Ringed Seal cannot tolerate the pressure at great sea depths, nor can it tolerate being without air for

RANGE: Ringed Seals are found in the polar seas from Point Barrow, Alaska, in the West to Labrador and Newfoundland in the East.

STATUS: Stable

TOTAL LENGTH: 4–5½ ft (1.2–1.7 m)

WEIGHT: 110–250 lb (50–110 kg)

much longer than 15 minutes. As a result, the Ringed Seal remains in shallower areas, while the Bearded Seal occupies deeper waters.

Although it spends most of its time in the water, the Ringed Seal digs small chambers under the snow, but above the ice, where it rests when it needs to reoxygenate its blood after long dives. Sometimes, many seals are found together in chambers that are connected by short passageways.

Walruses (p. 124), sharks and Orcas (p. 86) are the biggest threats to the Ringed Seal in the water, while Polar Bears, Arctic Foxes and humans are the dangerous creatures on the ice. There is no place where this seal is truly safe, and it seems to know it— every minute or so a Ringed Seal lifts its head to scan its surroundings for danger. Even in its snowy den, this seal is watchful and ready to flee a Polar Bear that has sniffed it out and dug through the snow to reach it. The Arctic Fox, which preys on the pups, is small enough to walk right in to the den.

The presence of PCBs and DDT in the environment is believed to have reduced the pregnancy rates of female Ringed Seals to as low as 28 percent in certain areas, and in combination with heavy losses from predation, and from hunting in some areas, these low fertility rates may threaten the survival of some local Ringed Seal populations.

DESCRIPTION: This little seal is one of the smallest aquatic carnivores. It reaches a maximum length of $5^1/_2$ ft (1.7 m), although it is usually only 4 ft (1.2 m) long. Its fur is variegated brown or even bluish black above and pale yellowish or gray below, with irregular doughnut-shaped rings of light-colored fur on the sides and back. It has long whiskers and eyebrows, a short muzzle and dark eyes. Males are typically larger than females.

HABITAT: The Ringed Seal spends most of its life underwater in the northern polar seas. It maintains breathing holes under the ice by digging the ice away with its sharp

REPRODUCTION: A female typically mates annually, in April or early May, and gives birth to a single pup the following March, after 11 months of gestation. The Ringed Seal is unique among seals because of the maternal den it constructs under the snow. A pregnant female may hollow out a shallow chamber in the snow above a breathing hole, or she may use a natural snow cave. Maternal chambers are typically about 7 x 10 ft (2 x 3 m) wide and only 2 ft (60 cm) deep. The young are born helpless, but with all their teeth, and covered in lanugo (the soft downy fur that is reminiscent of a white Teddy Bear). A pup nurses for about two months. When its mother leaves the den to feed, the pup remains by itself and waits quietly. Some pups may stay near their mothers for the remainder of the year, while other pups may disperse soon after weaning.

claws. This seal usually stays under or near landfast ice, and it is seldom seen on shifting or broken ice floes.

FOOD: In shallow water these seals feed mainly on shrimp, small fish and crustaceans. In deep water their diet shifts to larger zooplankton, such as amphipods.

Bearded Seal

SIMILAR SPECIES: Harbor Seal (p. 128); Bearded Seal (p. 140).

Ribbon Seal

Histriophoca fasciata

DESCRIPTION: Male and female Ribbon Seals differ slightly in their appearance: males, which are usually larger, are typically brown with cream-colored rings around the neck, rump and base of their front flippers; females have a similar pattern of less-distinct rings over a mainly gray body. The Ribbon Seal is unique among the true seals in that it moves by a slithering motion, instead of an inchworm or belly-flop motion, in which it throws its head and neck from side to side to alternately stretch forward its front flippers, which are used to pull itself along.

HABITAT: The Ribbon Seal is at home in cold arctic seas. It hauls out on ice floes to rest.

RANGE: Ribbon Seals are found in the Bering Sea from Alaska to the Aleutian Islands.

STATUS: Rare but stable

TOTAL LENGTH: 5–6 ft (1.5–1.8 m)

TOTAL WEIGHT: 180–200 lb (82–91 kg)

SEALS & OTTERS

FEEDING: Ribbon Seals feed mainly on fish (including eelpouts, capelin, pollack, sculpin and cod), octopus and shrimp. The adults fast during their reproductive and molting seasons.

REPRODUCTION: In late April, the female gives birth to a pup conceived the previous year, and soon after she mates again. Females give birth on ice floes, and they stay in the same site for about one month, until their pups are weaned. The pups are covered in white lanugo at first, which is replaced by a bluish coat after about five weeks. Their "ribbon" fur does not grow until their second year.

Harbor Seal

SIMILAR SPECIES: Harbor Seal (p. 128); Spotted Seal (p. 132).

Bearded Seal

Erignathus barbatus

The Bearded Seal is perhaps the most vocal of all seals—what it lacks in its nondescript appearance, it easily makes up for with its repertoire of unusual and haunting calls. In spring, the male Bearded Seal sings melodious yet eerie songs beneath the ice. Each song can last for up to a minute, and they carry for a long distance underwater. To court a female, a bull hauls out on the ice and serenades the cows with his echoing, warbling calls.

Bearded Seals can dive to a maximum depth of about 650 ft (200 m). Mammals that are not specialized for diving—such as humans—would suffer from the "bends" when descending to such depths and returning to the surface. The bends is a condition where nitrogen bubbles form in the blood as the pressure decreases: nitrogen already present in the blood may come out of solution, or expanding nitrogen from the lungs can transfer directly into the blood. This condition occurs when the body has adjusted to the great pressure underwater, and a rapid return to the surface reduces the pressure too quickly.

RANGE: Bearded Seals inhabit the northern coastal waters and shallow arctic seas from Point Barrow, Alaska, to Labrador.

STATUS: Stable

TOTAL LENGTH: 7–10 ft (2.1–3 m)

WEIGHT: 430–770 lb (200–350 kg)

Extensive research has been conducted to determine how certain species of seals can dive unharmed to such great depths. It turns out that before a dive, the seals breathe air out of their lungs, rather than into their lungs. The air they do retain is held in their windpipe. The windpipe is more rigid than the lungs and can tolerate the pressure changes of the dive. This unique method prevents the bends from occurring.

When humans hold their breath, the increasing carbon dioxide levels in the blood trigger them to breathe again in a very short time. This trigger is greatly desensitized in seals, and they are able to postpone breathing for about 30 minutes. When a seal is underwater, its nostrils are closed and its heartbeat is slowed from the normal 100 beats a minute to about 10 beats a minute. During the dive, the muscles function mainly anaerobically, creating an oxygen debt in the body.

Seals store oxygen in their blood and in certain molecules of the muscle itself, and this stored oxygen is used, or "spent," during the dive. The longer the dive lasts, the greater the body's oxygen debt becomes. When the dive is over, the seal must rest and rebuild, or "pay back," the oxygen stores of its body— when a Bearded Seal is basking, it is not just enjoying the sun, it is allowing its body to slowly reoxygenate after a long dive.

DESCRIPTION: As its name suggests, this seal has a beard of long, flat bristles on either side of the muzzle. Other seals have whiskers, but none compare to the long bristly beard of the Bearded Seal. Each long bristle is extremely sensitive, and together the bristles help the seal locate its favorite foods in mucky sea bottoms. The head of this large seal is noticeably small for its body size. The fur varies in color from uni-formly light brown to tawny golden to gray-ish. The front flippers are distinctively squarish, and the third digit is longer than all the rest. In a switch from many other pin-nipeds, female Bearded Seals are slightly larger than males.

HABITAT: The Bearded Seal spends most of its time in the water of cold arctic seas. It primarily stays in water no deeper than

Favorite foods include cod, sculpin, flounder, octopus and a variety of shellfish, such as whelks and clams.

REPRODUCTION: In May, the mating season is marked by these normally solitary seals forming groups of up to 50 individuals. The males are marvelously vocal, and they emit warbling calls on the ice surface to serenade the cows. Females are not vocal. Sometimes the bulls fight each other to establish hierarchy, but the dominant bulls do not form harems. A female gives birth on the ice to one young in April or May, after a gestation of about 11 months. The pup is well developed at birth and is nursed for no more than 18 days. The pup puts on blubber during this short nursing period and goes from weighing 70 lb (32 kg) at birth to about 200 lb (91 kg) by day 18, at which time the pup is weaned and the mother leaves.

500 ft (150 m), because it dives to the bottom to feed. The Bearded Seal is only rarely seen on land—it prefers open water and rests on drift ice and ice floes. This seal is not migratory, but it does follow the ice as it moves seasonally.

FOOD: Using its powerful claws and keenly sensitive whiskers, the Bearded Seal locates bottom-dwelling fish and shellfish to eat.

Ringed Seal

SIMILAR SPECIES: Ringed Seal (p. 134); Harbor Seal (p. 128).

Northern Elephant Seal

Mirounga angustirostris

The aptly named Northern Elephant Seal is one of the largest seals of all—only its Southern Hemisphere counterpart, the Southern Elephant Seal (*M. leonina*), is slightly larger.

The Northern Elephant Seal is an animal of superlatives, and it is also famous for its long migrations and incredible diving capabilities. The Northern Elephant Seal migrates twice a year, and some far-ranging males may cover 13,000 mi (21,000 km), which is even more than the renowned Gray Whale (p. 38), and spend more than 250 days at sea. When an elephant seal dives for food, it can remain submerged for 80 minutes and reach depths of up to 5000 ft (1500 m). Only the Sperm Whale (p. 110) and some of the beaked whales (pp. 100–7) can dive deeper or for longer.

Every year, sometime between December and March, adult Northern Elephant Seals arrive at sandy beaches in California or Mexico to give birth and mate. Northern

RANGE: These enormous seals are found from coastal Baja California to the Gulf of Alaska. They probably disperse a couple of hundred miles from the coast during the non-breeding season.

STATUS: Vulnerable but stable

TOTAL LENGTH: male 12–16 ft (3.7–4.9 m); female 7–12 ft (2.1–3.7 m)

TOTAL WEIGHT: male up to 2.5 tons (2300 kg); female 1 ton (910 kg)

SEALS & OTTERS

Elephant Seals are very noisy on land: the males produce a series of loud rattling snorts; the females make extremely inelegant sounds resembling monstrous belches. After pupping and mating, the adults and the young of the year depart for good feeding waters. Adult males and some juveniles may venture as far north as the Gulf of Alaska and the Aleutian Islands, where they feast on the abundant sea life. The females and most of the year's young do not travel quite as far: they prefer feeding in waters between 40° N and 45° N.

After feeding for two to five months, the Northern Elephant Seals return to the sandy shores of Mexico and California to molt sometime between April and August. When they molt, they shed their short, dense, yellowish-gray pelage along with large patches of old skin. During both the mating and molting seasons, elephant seals fast and lose up to 36 percent of their body weight. After the molting season, they once again venture out to food-rich waters to replenish their bodies before the mating season.

In the past, whalers frequently took high numbers of elephant seals in addition to their regular whale kills. This commercial harvest of elephant seals for oil reduced the worldwide population to between 100 and 1000 individuals, with some local populations completely extirpated. These seals are now fully protected under the U.S. Marine Mammal Protection Act, and their numbers have increased dramatically to a good population size. With increasing populations, more sightings off the British Columbia coast are being reported.

DESCRIPTION: Without a doubt, the sheer enormity of this creature gives away its identity. If you are in doubt, however, a closer look at its nose will be the confirmation: both sexes have a large nose that extends past the mouth, but adult males have a pendulous, inflatable, foot-long snout that resembles a trunk. This seal is mainly gray or light brown in color, with similarly colored sparse hair. Its hind flippers appear to be lobed on either side, and they have reduced claws. The tough skin of the male's neck and chest is covered with creases, scars and wrinkles, a feature absent in females. Pups are born black but molt to silver at one month.

HABITAT: The Northern Elephant Seal lives in temperate waters off the West Coast. It migrates between its northern feeding waters and southern breeding and molting beaches twice a year. During its molting and large fish. Adult males feed on larger prey than do the females and pups, and they typically migrate to more northern feeding grounds.

REPRODUCTION: The adults come ashore to give birth and mate sometime between December and March. These seals are polygamous, but not strongly territorial. Males arrive on shore first and battle fiercely for status in the social hierarchy. A high status means they can have a large harem. The females come ashore a couple of weeks after the males, and within a few days they may give birth to a pup conceived in the previous breeding season. The gestation period is 11 months. A female nurses her pup for no more than one month, during which time she fasts. Just a few days before her pup is to be weaned, she mates, and then, after she weans her pup, she leaves. Females are sexually mature at two to five years. Males typically cannot win a harem until they are 9 or 10 years old.

breeding seasons, the Northern Elephant Seal hauls out onto sandy beaches. It does not haul out onto rocks, but it may cross over rocks to reach a sandy beach. This seal rarely hauls out during the feeding season; instead, it can rest at the surface of the water, and it can stay offshore for weeks at a time.

FEEDING: Elephant seals feed on a variety of sea creatures, including squid, octopus, small sharks, rays, pelagic red crabs and

Walrus

SIMILAR SPECIES: Walrus (p. 124).

147

Sea Otter

Enhydra lutris

For many people, the playful and intelligent Sea Otter is among the most desired animals to see while visiting the West Coast. It has such a buoyant body and curious demeanor that watching it is not only comical but mesmerizing. When two Sea Otters are playing, they turn somersaults at the surface and wrestle together as if trying to dunk each other under. When they are resting, they lounge on their backs at the surface and rub their faces with curled-up paws, much like cats do when grooming. Sea Otters are even neighborly, and they regularly hobnob with the local sea-lions and seals.

The Sea Otter does not have a layer of insulating blubber like other marine mammals, and it relies on its high metabolism and thick coat to keep warm. Its full coat is both a blessing and a curse, however, because Sea Otters were hunted for their pelts almost to extinction. The otters that now inhabit the West Coast are probably all descendants of reintroduction programs that occurred in 1969. They now breed and are slowly increasing their numbers, but they are still vulnerable. Sea Otters can also be victims of oil spills, because the oil slicks their coat and destroys the insulating and water-proofing qualities of the fur. Otters caught in oil have extremely low chances of survival.

SEALS & OTTERS

RANGE: Sea Otters are found on the West Coast from southern California to the Aleutian Islands.

STATUS: Threatened (COSEWIC); once critically endangered, but some populations have recovered

TOTAL LENGTH: 30–60 in (76–152 cm)

TAIL LENGTH: 10–16 in (25–41 cm)

TOTAL WEIGHT: 50–100 lb (23–45 kg)

The Northern River Otter (p. 152) is the only animal you are likely to confuse with the Sea Otter, but the two are quite easy to tell apart—with the right information. Sea Otters do not venture more than 1 mi (1.6 km) out from shore, and they stay in water no more than 100 ft (30 m) deep. Typically,

they stay close to rocky shores, anywhere kelp beds are abundant. They also prefer open coastlines, and are therefore rarely seen along the Inside Passage. Northern River Otters, on the other hand, are frequently seen in the sheltered waters of the Inside Passage. Also, river otters are well-known for their travels, and an otter seen a few miles from shore, or that is swimming long distances from island to island, is most likely a Northern River Otter.

Anytime an otter is seen moving or eating on land, it is, again, a river otter. Sea Otters are very clumsy on land, and their locomotion is limited to an ungainly lope, an awkward walk or an even slower, body-dragging slide. Being so limited on land, the Sea Otter rarely comes out of the water, and only when a rough storm forces it out of its watery home.

DESCRIPTION: The stout-bodied Sea Otter has a short tail and a rounded head. Its slightly flattened tail is no more than one-third the length of its body. The fur may be a variety of colors, including light brown, reddish brown, yellowish gray or nearly black, and it is very thick, especially on the throat and chest. Folds of skin between the chest and each underarm form two pockets of skin. The head is often lighter than the body; in old males the head may be nearly white. The tiny ears may appear "pinched," but are otherwise inconspicuous. All four feet are webbed, and the hindlegs resemble flippers. Male Sea Otters are generally larger than females.

HABITAT: The Sea Otter lives almost its entire life at sea, only coming out onto rocks to rest during rough or stormy weather. It otter dives underwater for up to five minutes and returns to the surface with its prey and a stone, using the pockets of skin that run from its chest to its underarms to carry its load. One otter was once seen unloading six urchins and three oysters from her "cargo holds." To unload its pockets and eat, the otter rests on its back. It places the stone on its chest and uses it as an anvil on which to bash the shell of the urchin, shellfish or crustacean repeatedly until it breaks, exposing the flesh inside.

REPRODUCTION: Mating occurs in the water, usually in late summer. The female gives birth to one pup $6^1/2$ to 9 months later. As in many weasels, delayed implantation of the embryo is probably involved in the long gestation period. On rare occasions, a female can have two pups. She gives birth in the water, and to nurse her young, she floats on her back and allows the pup to sit on her chest. The pup also plays and naps on its mother's chest. It is weaned when it is one year old, but it may stay with its mother for several more months, even if she gives birth again. If the mother senses danger, such as an approaching shark or Orca (p. 86), she will hold her pup under her forelegs and dive into a kelp bed until the danger passes.

favors areas of kelp beds or reefs with nearby or underlying rocks. At night, or for daytime rest, a Sea Otter wraps itself in kelp at the surface. The kelp is attached underwater and prevents the otter from drifting while it sleeps. A Sea Otter is never more than 1 mi (1.6 km) from shore.

FEEDING: Sea Otters feed primarily on sea urchins, crustaceans, shellfish and fish. The

Northern River Otter

SIMILAR SPECIES:
Northern River Otter (p. 152).

Northern River Otter

Lontra canadensis

Many Northern River Otters live year-round on the coast, and enthusiastic wildlife watchers frequently mistake them for Sea Otters (p. 148). These two species have different appearances and preferred habitats, but they can be difficult to tell apart when they are seen in the water at a distance.

River otters can be active during day or night, but they tend to be more nocturnal where there is human activity. Their permanent dens are often in a bank, with both underwater and abovewater entrances.

DESCRIPTION: This large, weasel-like carnivore has a dark brown back that looks black when it is wet. It is paler below, and the throat is often silver gray. The head is broad and flattened, and it has small eyes, small ears and prominent, whitish whiskers. All four feet are webbed. The long tail is thick at the base and gradually tapers to the tip. Male river otters are larger than females.

HABITAT: River otters may visit coastal areas for brief periods, or they may live at the coast year-round. They sometimes roam

RANGE: The coastal range of the Northern River Otter extends from the Bering Strait to Northern California in the West and from Labrador to Texas in the East.

STATUS: Threatened

TOTAL LENGTH: 3 ½–4 ½ ft (1.1–1.4 m)

TAIL LENGTH: 12–20 in (30–51 cm)

TOTAL WEIGHT: 10–30 lb (4.5–14 kg)

SEALS & OTTERS

far from water, especially young males establishing new territories. When roaming, a river otter rests under roots or overhangs, in hollow logs, in the abandoned burrows of other mammals or in ledges on rocky outcroppings.

FEEDING: On the coast, river otters feed primarily on crabs, although fish and shellfish are eaten when available. These coastal otters occasionally eat small terrestrial animals, such as mice, insects and earthworms.

REPRODUCTION: The female bears a litter of one to six blind, fully furred young in March or April. The young are 140 g (5 oz) at birth. They first leave the den at three to four months, and leave their parents at six to seven months. River otters become sexually mature at two years. The mother breeds again soon after her litter is born, but delayed implantation of the embryos puts off the birth until the following spring.

Sea Otter

SIMILAR SPECIES: Sea Otter (p. 148).

Glossary

AMPHIPODS: a group of shrimp-like creatures, including krill, that are the primary food for many whale species.

BALEEN: long, thin plates of keratinous material that hang from the upper jaw in a baleen whale's mouth and are used for filter-feeding.

BULL: an adult male cetacean or pinniped.

CALF: a baby cetacean.

CALLOSITY: an area of skin that is hardened by growths of lumpy, keratinous material.

CETACEAN: referring to the order of animals (Cetacea) that encompasses all whale, dolphin and porpoise species.

COPEPODS: a large group of marine and aquatic crustaceans, including amphipods, that are the primary food for many marine creatures.

COSEWIC: Committee on the Status on Endangered Wildlife in Canada.

COW: an adult female cetacean or pinniped.

ECHOLOCATION: the detection of an object by emitting sounds waves and interpreting the returning echoes, which are changed from bouncing off the object.

ENDANGERED: facing imminent extirpation or extinction.

EXTIRPATED: no longer existing locally, but found elsewhere in the world.

FLUKE: the horizontally flattened tail of a cetacean.

FUSIFORM: spindle-shaped; having an elongated body that tapers at both ends.

KERATINOUS: referring to the material that composes hair, wool and nails in many mammals.

KRILL: a general name to describe more than 80 species of small, shrimp-like organisms that are eaten by numerous marine creatures.

LARYNGEAL: referring to the larynx in the region of the throat, which can be made to vibrate to produce sound.

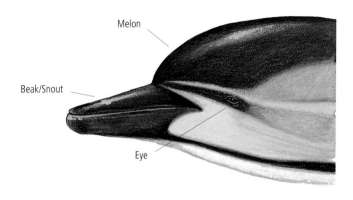

Melon

Beak/Snout

Eye

MIGRATION: the journey that an animal undergoes to get from one region to another, usually in response to seasonal and reproductive cycles.

MYSTICETES: all the cetaceans that have baleen instead of teeth.

NOMADIC: referring to creatures that move from region to region solely in response to food availability and that otherwise do not migrate.

ODONTOCETES: all the cetaceans that have teeth instead of baleen.

PELAGIC: living in the open sea far from land.

PINNIPEDIA: referring to the suborder of carnivores (order Carnivora) that encompasses all seals, sea-lions and walruses.

PLANKTON: the tiny plants (phytoplankton) and animals (zooplankton) that drift in the water column and are the base of the food chain.

PUP: a baby pinniped.

PURSE-SEINE: a type of long net (often more than 1 mi [1.6 km] long) that is set around a large shoal of fish and drawn up from the bottom ropes to create a "purse" that traps the fish.

RORQUAL: strictly a whale in the genus *Balaenoptera*; most authorities also include the Humpback Whale.

ROSTRUM: the forward-projecting snout of a cetacean.

SONAR: the ability to detect or track objects underwater by monitoring their sound emissions or how sound bounces off them.

STRANDING: an event where a cetacean comes onto land or shallow water and becomes stuck; the reasons for such occurrences are unknown.

THREATENED: likely to become endangered if limiting factors are not reversed.

ULTRASOUND: ultrasonic sound waves that can penetrate surfaces to register subsurface details.

VESTIGIAL: a part or organ of a creature that has atrophied or is rendered functionless by the process of evolution.

VULNERABLE: of special concern because of characteristics that make it particularly sensitive to human activities or natural events.

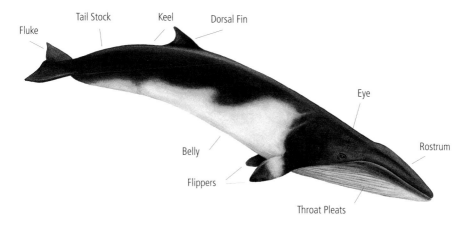

Fluke • Tail Stock • Keel • Dorsal Fin • Eye • Rostrum • Belly • Flippers • Throat Pleats

Whale Research, Conservation Groups and Further Reading

SOCIETIES AND ORGANIZATIONS

North Gulf Oceanic Society
P.O. Box 15244
Homer, Alaska 99603

Pratt Musuem
3779 Bartlett Street
Homer, Alaska 99603

Royal British Columbia Museum
672 Belleville Street
Victoria, B.C. V8V 1X4

Strawberry Island Research
P.O. Box 213
Tofino, B.C. V0R 2Z0

Vancouver Aquarium Marine Science Centre
Stanley Park
P.O. Box 3232
Vancouver, B.C. V6B 3X8
http://www.vanaqua.org/

Whale Centre
411 Campbell Street
P.O. Box 393
Tofino, B.C. V0R 2Z0

Wickaninnish Centre
Pacific Rim National Park
P.O. Box 280
Ucluelet, B.C. V0R 3A0

EMERGENCY CONTACTS IN BRITISH COLUMBIA

Whale Reporting and Stranding Report Line: (800) 665-5939
Marine Mammal Research Group: (250) 380-1925
Marine Mammal Harassment, Department of Fisheries and Oceans: (800) 465-4336

IN PRINT

Breton, M. 1986. *Guide to Watching Whales in Canada*. Department of Fisheries and Oceans, Ottawa.

Bulloch, D. K. 1993. *The Whaleswatcher's Handbook: A Guide to the Whales, Dolphins and Porpoises of North America*. Lyons and Burford, New York, New York.

Byrd, E. 1995. *The Hello Dolphin Project*. World Dolphin Project. Dolphin Assisted Therapy 1995 Symposium, Cancun.

Carwardine, M. 1995. *Whales, Dolphins and Porpoises*. Stoddart Publishing, Toronto.

Clapham, P. 1997. *Whales*. Raincoast Books, Vancouver.

Conner, R. C., and D. M. Peterson. 1994. *The Lives of Whales and Dolphins*. Henry Holt and Company, New York, New York.

Corrigan, P. 1991. *Where the Whales Are*. The Globe Pequot Press, Chester, Conneticut.

Darling, J. D., C. Nicklin, K. S. Norris, H. Whitehead and B. Würsig. 1995. *Whales, Dolphins and Porpoises*. National Geographic Society, Washington, D.C.

Flaherty, C. 1990. *Whales of the Northwest*. Cherry Lane Press, Seattle.

Gordon, D. G., and C. Flaherty. 1990. *Field Guide to the Orca*. Sasquatch Books, Seattle.

Hoyt, E. 1984. *The Whales of Canada*. Camden House Publishing, Camden East, Ontario.

Kaiper, D., and N. Kaiper. 1978. *Tlingit: Their Art, Culture and Legends*. Hancock House Publishers, Saanichton, British Columbia.

Mason, A. 1999. *Whales, Dolphins and Porpoises*. Altitude Publishing, Canmore, Alberta.

Reader's Digest. 1997. *Reader's Digest Explores Whales, Dolphins and Porpoises*. The Reader's Digest Association, Pleasantville, New York.

Spalding, D.A.E. 1998. *Whales of the West Coast*. Harbour Publishing, Madeira Park, British Columbia.

Stewart, F., et al. *The Presence of Whales*. Whitecap Books, Vancouver/Toronto, Canada.

Stonehouse, B. 1998. *A Visual Introduction to Whales, Dolphins and Porpoises*. Checkmark Books, New York, New York.

ONLINE

AMERICAN CETACEAN SOCIETY
http://www.acsonline.org/

CETACEA
http://www.cetacea.org/

COMMITTEE ON THE STATUS OF ENDANGERED WILDLIFE IN CANADA (COSEWIC)
http://www.cosewic.gc.ca/COSEWIC/

CONVENTION ON INTERNATIONAL TRADE OF ENDANGERED SPECIES OF WILD FLORA AND FAUNA (CITES)
http://www.wcmc.org.uk/CITES/eng/index.shtml

DOLPHIN RESEARCH CENTER
http://www.dolphins.org/

DOLPHIN INSITUTE
http://www.dolphin-institute.com/

EARTHFILES
http://www.earthfiles.com/

INSTITUTE OF CETACEAN RESEARCH
http://www.whalesci.org/

INTERNATIONAL MARINE MAMMAL PROJECT
http://www.earthisland.org/immp/index.html

OCEAN LINK
http://www.oceanlink.island.net/olink.html

PROJECT AWARE
(Aquatic World Awareness, Responsibility and Education)
http://www.padi.com/

SEAL CONSERVATION SOCIETY
http://www.greenchannel.com/tec/species/

SHEDD AQUARIUM
http://www.sheddnet.org/

WHALE AND DOLPHIN CONSERVATION SOCIETY
http://www.wdcs.org/wdcs/index.htm

WHALENET
http://whale.wheelock.edu/

WHALES ON THE NET: LATEST NEWS
http://www.magna.com.au/NEWS/

Index

Page numbers in **boldface** type refer to the primary account for a species.

Balaena
  australis, 37, 58
  glacialis, **58–61**
  mysticetus, **62–63**
Balaenoptera
  acutorostrata, **42–45**
  borealis, **46–47**
  musculus, **50–53**
    intermedia, 51
    brevicauda, 51
  physalus, **48–49**
Beaked Whale
  Baird's, **100–1**
  Bering Sea. *See* Stejneger's B. W.
  Cuvier's, **102–3**
  Hubbs's, **104–5**
  North Pacific. *See* Stejneger's B. W.
  Stejneger's, **106–7**
Beluga, **66–69**
Berardius bairdii, **100–1**
Blackfish. *See* Whale, False Killer; Pilot Whale,
  Short-finned

Cachalot. *See* Whale, Sperm
Callorhinus ursinus, **116–17**

Delphinapterus leucas, **66–69**
Delphinus spp., **72–75**
  capensis, 72
  delphis, 72
Devilfish. *See* Whale, Gray
Dolphin
  Common. *See* Saddleback D.
  Criss-cross. *See* Saddleback D.
  Hook-finned. *See* Pacific White-sided D.
  Northern Right Whale, **90–91**
  Pacific Striped. *See* Pacific White-sided D.
  Pacific White-sided, **76–79**
  Risso's, **80–81**
  Saddleback, **72–75**
    Long-beaked, 72
    Short-beaked, 72
  Striped, **70–71**
  White-striped. *See* Pacific White-sided D.

Elephant Seal
  Northern, **144–47**
  Southern, 144
Enhydra lutris, **148–51**
Erignathus barbatus, **140–43**
Eschrichtius robustus, **38–41**
Eumetopias jubatus, **118–21**

Finback. *See* Whale, Fin
  Lesser. *See* Whale, Minke
Finner. *See* Whale, Fin
  Japan. *See* Whale, Sei
  Little. *See* Whale, Minke
  Sharp-headed. *See* Whale, Minke

Globicephala macrorhynchus, **84–85**
Grampus griseus, **80–81**

Histriophoca fasciata, **138–39**

Kogia sima, **108–9**

Lag. *See* Dolphin, Pacific White-sided
Lagenorhynchus obliquidens, **76–79**
Lissodelphis borealis, **90–91**
Lontra canadensis, **152–53**

Megaptera novaeangliae, **54–57**
Mesoplodon
  carlhubbsi, **104–5**
  stejnegeri, **106–7**
Mirounga
  angustirostris, **144–47**
  leonina, 144
Mussel-digger. *See* Whale, Gray

Odobenus rosmarus, **124–27**
Orca, 39, 73, 76, **86–89**, 97, 135
Orcinus orca, **86–89**
Otter
  Northern River, 149, **152–53**
  Sea, **148–51**, 152

Phoca
  largha, **132–33**
  vitulina, **128–31**
Phocoena phocoena, **92–95**
Phocoenoides dalli, **96–99**
Physeter macrocephalus, **110–13**
Pilot Whale
  False. *See* Whale, False Killer
  Pacific. *See* Short-finned P. W.
  Short-finned, **84–85**
Porpoise
  Common. *See* Harbor P.
  Dall's, **96–99**
  Harbor, **92–95**
  Pacific Right Whale. *See* Dolphin, Northern
    Right Whale
  Puffing. *See* Harbor P.
  Spray. *See* Dall's P.
  True's. *See* Dall's P.
  White-flanked. *See* Dall's P.
Pseudorca crassidens, **82–83**
Pseudorca. *See* Whale, False Killer
Pusa hispida, **134–37**

Razorback. *See* Whale, Fin
Right Whale
  Biscayan. *See* Northern R. W.
  Black. *See* Northern R. W.
  Northern, **58–61**
  Southern, 58
Rorqual
  Boreal. *See* Whale, Sei
  Common. *See* Whale, Fin
  Great Northern. *See* Whale, Blue
  Lesser. *See* Whale, Minke
  Rudolphi's. *See* Whale, Sei
  Sibbald's. *See* Whale, Blue

Sea Canary. *See* Beluga
Seal. *See also* Elephant Seal
  Bearded, **140–43**
  Harbor, 118, **128–31**
  Northern Fur, **116–17**
  Ribbon, **138–39**
  Ringed, **134–37**
  Spotted, **132–33**
Sea-Lion
  California, 119, **122–23**
  Northern, **118–21**, 122
  Steller. *See* Northern S.-L.

Stenella coeruleoalba, **70–71**
Sulfur-bottom. *See* Whale, Blue

Walrus, **124–27**, 135
  Atlantic, 125
  Pacific, 125
Whale. *See also* Beaked Whale; Pilot Whale;
    Right Whale
  Anvil-headed. *See* Sperm W.
  Arch-beaked. *See* Beaked Whale, Hubbs's
  Blue, **50–53**, 59
    Pygmy, 51
  Bowhead, **62–63**
  Coalfish. *See* Sei W.
  Cuvier's. *See* Beaked Whale, Cuvier's
  Dwarf Sperm, **108–9**
  False Killer, **82–83**
  Fin, 46, **48–49**
  Giant Bottlenosed. *See* Beaked Whale,
    Baird's
  Giant Four-toothed. *See* Beaked Whale,
    Baird's
  Goose-beaked. *See* Beaked Whale, Cuvier's
  Gray, **38–41**
  Herring. *See* Fin W.
  Humpback, **54–57**, 76, 82
  Killer. *See* Orca
  Minke, **42–45**
  North Pacific Great Bottlenosed. *See* Beaked
    Whale, Baird's
  Northern Four-toothed. *See* Beaked Whale,
    Baird's
  Piked. *See* Minke W.
  Pollack. *See* Sei W.
  Pothead. *See* Short-finned Pilot W.
  Sabre-toothed. *See* Beaked Whale, Stejneger's
  Sardine. *See* Sei W.
  Scrag. *See* Gray W.
  Sei, **46–47**
  Sperm, **110–13**
  White. *See* Beluga

Zalophus californianus, **122–23**
Ziphius cavirostris, **102–3**